Thank you ~ ... phone. I was ... some good person would find it.

Blessings,
Phil

# on
# the
# way
# to
# here

*The Devlin homestead where my mother was born in 1898*

# on the way to here

*Reflections on Things that Matter*

## Phil Small

FriesenPress

FriesenPress

Suite 300 - 990 Fort St
Victoria, BC, V8V 3K2
Canada

www.friesenpress.com

ISBN
978-1-4602-9802-2 (Hardcover)
978-1-4602-9803-9 (Paperback)
978-1-4602-9804-6 (eBook)

*1. SELF-HELP, MOTIVATIONAL & INSPIRATIONAL*

Distributed to the trade by The Ingram Book Company

For Margaret

Michelle and Bart, Christine, Jim

Emma, Leo, Owen, Quinn

In memory of Jim and Bessie

Ginny, Rita, Sylvia

# Contents

*I* had no idea that a phone conversation in May 1994 would lead to a book twenty-three years later. My friend Diane said at one point, "That doesn't sound like you. You're putting yourself down." I still do not know what prompted her to say that, but I pondered her comment for a couple of days and then wrote the reflection that I call my signature piece. "In Response to a Comment from Diane" has been its only title all these years.

> Two tiny particles of matter find their way to one another ... and I begin. I cross the chasm from nothingness to being. This was my only chance at existence. I have won the greatest lottery of all.

> Called by Life to the banquet of all that is. Called, however, to more than simple being. Called to know. And to know that I know. Called to love. And to know that I love.

> When did I first know that I am me? Was it the same day that I knew that you are you? What a comfort it was to realize that I am not alone.

> The whole journey has been one long introduction to myself. At first I was not sure that I wanted to be this one. Why couldn't I be that one? Or that one? Somewhere on the way to here I decided to be me. I even became excited about being me. I came to love this intense, introverted, extroverted, shy, gregarious human being who never ceases to be amazed that there is life, and who is so profoundly grateful that he was invited to the feast.

> Thank you, God, for me.

The thoughts expressed in this short piece must have come from some deep place inside me. The words have stayed with me ever since, and I have shared them verbally with numerous friends and even total strangers. People I had never met before have requested a copy. And so many of them have asked, "Has that been published?"

However, you do not publish a book because of one short piece of writing. That piece was followed by so many others. Over these past twenty-three years, most of them in retirement, I have written reflections on a wide variety of subjects, and I have sent letters to friends that often touched on matters of universal interest and concern. Though these reflections and letters were not written with publication in mind, a growing number of people have been telling me that they should be put into a book. It has taken me a long time to agree with them. You may decide if they were right.

An innate philosophical bent, plus several courses in philosophy and theology, have left me with a preoccupation with the spiritual dimension of life, and this comes through very naturally in my writing. I cannot write without wanting to get below the surface level to the deeper realities that we can so easily miss. The good stuff is there if we pause long enough to taste and relish it. Some people tell me that I manage to put into words things they feel at times but cannot fully express. It makes me happy to be able to do that for them. We all have different gifts—gifts that we are meant to share.

In his book *Report to Greco*, Nikos Kazantzakis writes: "Blowing through heaven and earth, and in our hearts and the heart of every living thing, is a gigantic breath—a great Cry—which we call God."[1] I think of that breath as the Source of all the creativity in humankind. The breath and the Cry are there in all of us. We give expression to them in our own unique ways, often unaware that we are.

If any words of mine hold special meaning for you, please direct your thanks to the One from whom the breath and all other gifts come.

---

1  Nikos Kazantzakis, *Report to Greco* (New York: Simon and Schuster, Inc., 1965), p. 278.

*I* wrote these various reflections because some special occasion, or a comment from a friend, or some cherished memory prompted me to write them. There was something inside me that wanted out, some story that wanted to be told, some feeling that wanted to be expressed. In a few cases, I wrote in response to a request to compose a piece for a wedding service or to help say goodbye to a dear family member.

The same is true of the letters included in this collection. They were certainly not written to be published. They are here only because they contain thoughts that may hold meaning for others as well. I am grateful to these friends for having agreed to allow me to publish what was written just for them. In a few cases I have deleted or changed names.

It feels a bit strange, and somewhat intimidating, to be putting some of my most personal thoughts out there for anyone at all to read. Some of you I know; we are friends. Others I will never know. I would much prefer to have met each of you in some natural way along life's path, to have become friends, to have shared a meal and exchanged our views on life. Every one of you is my brother or my sister on our common journey. And I hope that somewhere in these brief selections you will come across a piece that inspires or affirms you as you walk your own road.

In our later years our hearts and our minds bring us back to earlier times, and to life lessons we may not have realized we were acquiring. We draw our water from the well of the persons we have become. So it will be no surprise to those who know me that I write from a Catholic Christian perspective. That is the faith in which I was raised, and it is the faith that I later internalized and made my own, though not without serious doubts and deep anguish at times. I hope, however, that all of you who read these pages will see yourselves here in some real way, whatever religious views you may or may not hold. At some deep level we are all one. I cannot say even the first two words of the prayer Jesus taught us without being reminded of that.

The topics covered in this book are as varied as the occasions and the memories that prompted them. You will find here references to our first steps onto the human stage and thoughts relating to the day we take leave of this place. Plus reflections on much of what makes up our lives between those two poles: birth, childhood, friendship, love, marriage, special times in the year, significant people or events—and through all of this the unending search for the meaning that brings joy and purpose to our days. Socrates said that the unexamined life is not worth living. I am forever turning over the stones of our lives and looking for the meaning underneath.

It would be a mistake to pick up this book and read it through from beginning to end. This is not a novel. These reflections are meant to be savoured two or three at a time. They are the result of my tendency to ponder. They invite you to ponder as well.

You may notice that the title of the book appears in my signature piece. We are always "on the way to here." Hopefully, we will never stop growing, changing, becoming. That we will always be today in some way different than we were yesterday: more passionately engaged with life, more loving, more one with God and others. More *here*. Yet fully aware that 'here' is not a place to stay.

# Part 1

*Moments on the Journey*

# Observing

You told me that you sometimes like to sit there and simply observe the things around you. So how could I not think of you when I read the following account this morning?

In *Lost in Wonder*, Esther de Waal tells how Thomas Merton, the Trappist monk, once told a friend "to stop looking and to begin *seeing*" (her italics). Then she quotes Merton: "Because looking means that you already have something in mind for your eye to find; you've set out in search of your desired object and have closed off everything else presenting itself along the way. But seeing is being open and receptive to what comes to the eye; your vision total and not targeted."[2]

I immediately pictured you sitting there, slowly taking in the objects that surrounded you. You let your gaze fall on each one as you took the time *to see*. You said yes, one by one, to the light from each thing your eyes fell on and took it into yourself. Acknowledged its existence. Saw that it, too, is here. Reverenced its place in the universe.

There was a tender beauty in this scene. The things we call inanimate were being given voice, and were sensing that they too are loved. Just because they *are*. Each with its own right to be here. And the one doing the seeing was nourishing her own soul with *wonder*.

My heart warmed at the thought of my friend communing with her fellow creatures.

*February 28, 2011*

---

2  Ron Seitz, *Song for Nobody, A Memory Vision of Thomas Merton* (Ligouri, Missouri: Triumph Books, 1993), pp. 133-4.

# Aren't You Glad

"Jimmy, aren't you glad you were born? Isn't it great to be alive!" There was such sincerity in the old man's voice as he spoke these words to the one-year-old sitting in front of him on the kitchen floor. It almost seemed as though his great-nephew could understand what he was saying. Each was looking so intently at the other.

How had this uncle of mine preserved such immense enthusiasm for life in the face of all the misfortune he had known? He was only eleven when he and his three brothers and his sister lost the second of their parents. They would grow up in poverty as their maternal grandmother did her best to keep them all together. The young woman he later fell in love with had chosen to marry someone else. He would go out west on the top of a freight train during the Great Depression to see if he could find work. The fine woman he did eventually marry was taken from him only seven years later. He had withdrawn his few shares in a mining company before he would have come into some money. On one tragic evening he had held his dying brother in his arms as he bled to death from a gunshot wound. So many things had gone wrong. Yet here he was, close to ninety, and still grateful for the gift of life. Wanting to make sure that this little boy who could not yet speak knew how wonderful it was to have been born.

Was it his faith in God that had kept him sane and grateful to be alive during all these years? He did tell us that even in his old age he still got down on his knees every morning and said the prayer his grandfather had taught him, asking God "to keep me a good boy today and every day." That prayer had certainly been answered.

*January 27, 2016*

"*A*untie Meaghan, am I inside myself?" What an amazing question, Nick, especially for a four-year-old! There are people much older than you who should be asking themselves that same question. It seems that you are already beginning to realize that you are more than this body you usually think of as yourself. You sense in some way that the "I" who asks if he is inside himself must somehow *be* his body but also be more than his body. I hope you always have this awareness and that it deepens as you grow older.

Your question opens up another whole way of looking at ourselves. Many, many years ago a very wise man said, "God is at home; it is we who have gone out for a walk." This was his way of saying that the God who made us dwells in the deepest and truest part of us, but that sometimes we are absent from ourselves. And, therefore, from God. We have walked away from what is most essential in us, the longing of our hearts for goodness and for living the way God wants us to live. Strange as it may seem, when we do that we are in some way no longer inside ourselves where we are meant to be. We have let our hearts go running after things that are bad for us and that take us away from ourselves at the same time as they take us away from God. There are all kinds of ways of doing this. When you are older you will see that some people turn money into their god. They just want to get very, very rich and they don't care how they do that. If the only way they can become rich is by hurting other people, then that's what they do. And if they succeed in becoming rich they just keep everything for themselves and refuse to help those who are in need. Money means everything to them. It is their god.

There are other ways too of making things, and sometimes even people, into gods. And every time we do that we move away from ourselves in some way. One of the saddest things is that we may not even know we are no longer fully inside ourselves because false gods have a way of fooling us. But if you stay close to the only God there is, as you grow up you will have a way of telling when you have "gone out for a walk." Because you will know that you are no longer "inside yourself," that something isn't right, that you don't feel good about yourself. You have wandered away from home, from God who lives inside you. And in some real sense you have wandered away from yourself. From the self who is made in the image and likeness of God. If that ever happens, just turn around and go back home. Home to your true self. And to God who is always there inside you to welcome you back.

My prayer for you, Nick, is that you spend your whole life "inside yourself."

God bless you, little one.
Phil

*March 26, 2009*

# A Manner of Speaking

*A* colleague and I were having lunch in the teachers' staffroom when she suddenly said, "Ouch, I bit my tongue." For some strange reason I immediately found myself wondering why we say *my* tongue? Why this possessive form of speech in reference to a part of our body? Did she give herself that tongue? How did she get to own it? Oh, I know we all talk this way, but is it an accurate way of speaking?

*My* leg, *my* knee, *my* shoulder, *my* neck. The fingers that are typing these words, don't I call them *my* fingers? From head to foot we talk this way. Okay, so these parts of this body don't belong to someone else. Why shouldn't I call them mine? I have every right to call them mine. I do. And yet...if I really didn't give them to myself, and if my parents didn't give them to me either, if we are going to be honest about it, then is there some sense in which they aren't, strictly speaking, mine after all? I hesitate before responding. I don't want to give away the farm here. How did I acquire them, these various organs and limbs that go to make up my physical being?

Should I simply accept Psalm 139:13: "For you formed my inward parts; you knitted me together in my mother's womb"? Makes more sense than any other explanation I've come across. I will continue to refer to *my* hand and *my* foot, but with the awareness that that's simply a manner of speaking.

*February 22, 2002*

$M$y dear friend,

"Thinking about what really matters... Beneath everything, what really matters to you?" You pose such interesting questions on Twitter.

Eight or nine years ago, when I was taking a theology course out of personal interest, I was assigned a spiritual director. That was one of the requirements for taking this particular course. I happened to have this Scottish nun as my spiritual director for the year. She had just come to Canada to teach theology at Regis College, one of the colleges attached to the University of Toronto. I met with her for an hour every second week.

A few months into our time together she asked me this question: "What is your deepest desire?" I thought for a few moments and then said, "To have all my loves be one Love." I think my response was influenced in some way by a quotation from Teilhard de Chardin, who wrote at the beginning of one of his books, "*Tout ce qui monte converge.*" ("All things which rise come together.") I pictured a triangle where everything from below was moving upward and, of course, meeting at the top. For me the top was God, and I pictured all things moving inexorably towards God, their final destination. That was how I wanted everything in me to be. I wanted all the scattered elements in my mind and heart to be flowing in this one direction. I wanted my love for Margaret, my love for our children, for my family of birth, for all my friends, for everyone I ever meet, to be all in harmony with one another and to be part of my overriding love for God. I wanted no love in my life that would be pulling me away in any manner from this upward movement towards my final destiny in God. The Danish philosopher Kierkegaard has as the title of one of his books *Purity of Heart Is to Will One Thing*. I love that title and wish I could arrive at that point: to will only one thing. To have everything in me and everything I do be part of my love for God. Talk about having it together! Wouldn't that be great? I imagine that is how the saints lived. Though they did not arrive there without years of doing their utmost to focus their lives on God, letting God lead them. Someone has said that the only tragedy is not to be a saint. It's hard to argue with that.

Someday I will close my eyes for the last time. I try to remind myself that what will matter then is what matters now. You may have seen the quotation "The most important things in life aren't things." (Bought a small ceramic plaque recently with that on it. Still have to hang it up.) I love our sailboat. It brings a great deal of pleasure to Margaret and me. And to our friends. But it is only a *thing*, after all, and it can never be more important than the people in my life. It is my love for them that I will take with me at the end. And my love for God's little ones, those who have so much less than we do. They have a claim on my love too. Finally, it's all about love, isn't it? When it comes right down to it, we are here to love and to be loved. How well I have loved will be what matters at the end. And is, therefore, what matters now.

Thank you, Meaghan, for inviting me to dwell on these things "that really matter" this morning. Just writing about these questions makes me want to try to live more deeply the reality of why we are here. Writing about them is one thing. I need to live them.

I find myself wanting to add now that all of this is more God's work in us than our own doing, though we obviously have our part. There was a time in my younger years when I was way too uptight about all of this. God wants cheerful children, not people with long faces going around trying to be holy. As I said in "New Year's Wish" that I wrote a year and a half ago, anxious striving does not help. What we need to do is be vigilant about what we love. For we become what we love. Loving God, and all people and things in God, is the very best thing we can do for these poor hearts of ours.

I love your question and I love you,
Phil

*April 29, 2010*

# Cursillo Witness Talk

*T*his past July I went into Toronto to see a young man who had just graduated from high school and would be going off to university in the fall. He wanted to talk about his difficulties at home and his hopes and fears about moving away and being on his own. So we got together for lunch. I was impressed with his intelligence and genuine love and admiration for his parents, despite the conflicts he sometimes experienced living with his family. Just last week I sent him this note to wish him well as he left for university.

"I know how eager you have been to reach this stage of your life. There have been times when it could not come soon enough. Now the time is here. Go with confidence into the future. You have a lot going for you: a fine mind, good health, excellent personal qualities. Be your own best friend and create the daily structure you will need to make the most of the opportunity that is before you now. I say 'structure' because you will need to have some order in your life if you want to be able to perform at your best. Doing things only when we 'feel like doing them' doesn't get most of us very far. At seventy-eight I still struggle at times to create a schedule for myself, to prioritize things, so that I don't arrive at the end of the day feeling I've wasted my time. If there's something I don't really want to do, but should do, I've learned that that is probably what I should do first. Once that's done I feel good about myself and have more energy for the other things.

"Feeling good about yourself is not a bad guide as you decide how to live your life. By now, Gabe, you have a good sense of what makes you truly happy as opposed to what simply gives you pleasure. Many of us forget that our first relationship is the one we have with ourselves. We lose sight of the fact that we have to make good decisions for this person inside our own skin, the only one we truly live with 24/7. The one whose approval we most need. The best advice I can give you, Gabe, is this: be good to yourself. Good in the deepest and truest sense of that lovely word. Do the things that will make you proud of you. Those are the same things that will make others proud of you. Including God. Who, of course, is always proud of us, even when we mess up."

It often happens that when I am giving advice to someone, I am really talking to myself as well. I am speaking out of my own need, of my awareness of some message that I need to hear too. That was certainly the case in my note to Gabe. When I said to him, "Be good to yourself...good in the deepest and truest sense of that word," I was thinking of the definition of love of St. Thomas Aquinas: "Love is willing good to another." Doesn't sound very romantic, does it? And yet, as I used to tell my students, if the "willing good" is not there, whatever else is there without that is not love. That is how I need to love myself, and it's not the same as pleasing myself, doing just whatever I feel like doing. In reality, willing good to myself will sometimes mean doing exactly the opposite of what I feel like doing.

You probably noticed that I focused on Gabe's relationship with himself. Over the past several years, I have become increasingly aware that the journey home to God and the journey home to ourselves are one and the same journey. And I keep coming across things that confirm this for me. Richard Rohr, the Franciscan priest who founded the Center For Action and Contemplation in New Mexico, says in his book *Everything Belongs*, "St. Augustine connects the inner journey with the journey toward God." Then he quotes from Augustine's Confessions: "I was admonished to return to my own self, and with You to guide me, I entered into the innermost part of myself, and I was able to do this because You were my helper." In his Soliloquies, Augustine addresses God with these words: "I did not find You without, Lord, because I wrongly sought You without, Who were within..."[3]

Another place in his book, Richard Rohr recounts the experience he had when he returned to the Trappist monastery in Kentucky to spend time in a hermitage. On earlier visits he learned that one of the former abbots had become a hermit and was spending all his time in the forest alone with God. Here is the surprise encounter Rohr had one day during his time of retreat: "I was going down a little trail from my hermitage, and I saw him (the former abbot) coming toward me. I recognized him since I knew him from years before. I felt it was not my place to intrude on his privacy or silence, so I bowed my head, moved to the side of the path and was going to walk past him.

---

3   Richard Rohr, *Everything Belongs* (New York: The Crossroad Publishing Company, 1999), p. 160.

When he was about four feet from me, he stopped and said, 'Richard, you get chances to preach and I don't. When you are...preaching, just tell the people one thing: God is not out there. God bless you.' And he went on down the road."[4]

God is not 'out there.' There are many ways of saying that. One of my favourite quotations is a simple but profound statement by Meister Eckhart, a Dominican theologian and mystic who lived around the year 1300. He said, "God is at home; it is we who have gone out for a walk." You and I know when we have 'gone out for a walk.' I know when I have not been true to myself. How I feel in some way estranged from my own inner person when I have done wrong, when I have sinned, when I have failed to love. Whether it was an unkind word I wish I had not spoken or something far more serious, I know that when I betray God I betray myself. And when I betray my best self I betray God. I cannot escape the fact that I carry that image and likeness in the very core of my being. As some spiritual writers remind us, God is more present to us than we are to our own selves. In a New Year's message I sent out to my friends a couple of years ago, I wrote: "Go forth to meet yourself each day, confident that on that same road you will meet Another who dwells in the deepest and most authentic part of you. Grow in the direction of that inner Presence." Once more I was speaking to myself too. I believe that with each step the prodigal son took on his homeward journey, he was returning to himself as well as to his father. The God who longs for our return waits there inside our own hearts. With arms outstretched.

De Colores!

*September 10, 2011*

---

4  Rohr, op. cit., p. 118.

# A Trinity of Thoughts

*I* spent last Tuesday in mourning. Mourning what seems at times like the loss of our son. Our only son. We had returned late Monday from visiting Jim in Texas, and I had to accept once more that he will probably never move back to Canada, that he will never again live anywhere near us. I had already accepted that (it's been almost two years since he moved there), but on Tuesday I had to accept it all over again. He is where he needs to be and that is where I want him. But it hurts in some ways.

Then on Wednesday a friend confided to me that she has begun to wean her ten-month-old son and that she is finding this emotionally difficult. He is their third child. Perhaps she will never again know the deep joy of holding her own flesh and blood to her breast. Nourishing out of her very substance the one she carried for months so near to her loving heart. How can she let go of this intimacy, of the comfort they both derive from this closeness?

Was it all this pondering the mystery of letting go that gave rise on Friday to a question I had never had before? Did God mind letting His Son go? Did He mind letting Him become one of us? Did even God find letting go difficult? "Heavenly Father, did you waver, even for a moment, torn between your infinite love for your Son and your infinite love for us? Was there any hesitation? Did the Eternal Word say, 'Father, please send me. You know how much We love them, even in their sin'? And did the Spirit say, 'I will be with Him at every moment till He returns to Us in glory'? Did it work like that? Forgive my foolish questions. I know your ways are so far beyond our ways. All I can say is, 'I love You. Help me to love You more and more.'"

*March 28, 2010 (Passion Sunday)*

# My Night in Jail

*I*t was Remembrance Day 1982. A Thursday. Back then there was a school holiday on Remembrance Day, and that meant I was free to join the others who planned to block the entrance to Litton Industries in Downsview. If they were going to continue to build the guidance system for the cruise missile, one equipped with a nuclear warhead in those days, then we would do our best to shut them down. At the very least, we would draw attention to the enterprise they were engaged in.

You need to understand that in 1982 the scientists had placed the hands of the Doomsday Clock at three minutes to midnight. That indicated their view of the likelihood of nuclear war between the United States and the Soviet Union. Many said that with so many nuclear warheads stockpiled on both sides, the chance of nuclear war starting by accident was almost as great as one being declared. Millions of people in those countries would almost certainly die, and millions more around the world would perish as well. You cannot tell clouds of radioactive materials to stay within specified borders. Some scientists wondered if a nuclear holocaust might not mean the end of all life on Earth.

A student wrote an article for the school newspaper in which he had the vice-principal announcing over the PA one morning that nuclear missiles were on their way to North America and would arrive in Toronto in twenty minutes. No one ridiculed his article as absurd. When the world's scientists had given their view of how dire the situation was, no student was going to be laughed at for describing an all-too-plausible scenario. Yet most of us went calmly about our day-to-day business. How else could one live but in denial of what was too unthinkable to contemplate? Collective insanity is not easy to live with. Best to pretend that all would be well.

During that year Margaret and I belonged to a group called Christian Initiative for Peace. We were about forty people of different Christian traditions who met in a United Church once a week to pray for peace and to strategize around the question of how to prevent nuclear war. We raised money to send delegations to Washington and Moscow to meet with members of government and peace groups in those two countries. We had no illusions that we would easily convince those in power to lay down their arms, especially their most fearful and destructive ones. Some local action would be needed as well to draw attention to our government that what was going on in our own country, in our own city, was both immoral and criminal. We were complicit in this mindless rush towards mutual destruction. Why not point out, in as dramatic a way as possible, that we were a part of this global madness?

So on Thursday, November 11, 1982, a number from our group joined with others of like mind, and over fifty of us sat down on the road and blocked the entrance to Litton Industries. We would use our bodies to say no to this insanity. Someone must have notified the police of our intentions because we were not sitting there very long before we were physically hauled away to the other side of the street. However, as soon as the police retreated to their earlier positions, we stood up and walked right back to once again block the entrance. This time we were given a different treatment. There was nothing gentle about the way we were hauled off this time. That November morning was a fairly cool one, and the heavy coat I was wearing was almost ripped off me by the burly police officer who was determined to show us that they meant business this time. There would be no third chance to block the entrance. We were now under arrest.

I forget how many we were in the paddy wagon. What I do remember is that I was right up against the screen that separated us from the police officers in the front seat. The driver had gone to speak to someone, and I struck up a conversation with the other officer who was sitting there waiting for him to return. I have always had this tendency to enter into conversation with total strangers, and I saw no reason not to continue this custom. He seemed quite willing to find out more about this forty-eight-year-old gentleman who appeared to be well spoken and not at all unpleasant. His shock was clearly evident when he learned that I taught religious studies in a Catholic high school. This was not the kind of activity that he imagined a teacher to be engaged in, and certainly not one who taught religion. By now I was glad that the other officer was being delayed and we had more time to chat. The tone became almost friendly. I took the opportunity to explain to him that, as much as I respected the laws of our country, there is a higher law than the ones we humans make. Our complicity in the planned mass murder of millions of our fellow human beings was so immoral that we had to stand against it. Nothing could justify this. Besides, this kind of warfare would not protect us and our children. We would all die in a nuclear holocaust. He seemed to have no answer to the points I was making and finally said, "Well, the day the pope does something like this, that's when I'll join in." At that moment I suspected that he was Catholic and that somehow I had touched his conscience. I have always regretted not making further contact with him after he very willingly gave me his badge number and the station he worked out of.

So off we went to be fingerprinted and taken to various jail cells across the city. When you have almost sixty people who decide to break the law at the same time, it can be a challenge to find accommodation for them all—especially if you want to send them to different places so they can't collaborate and plan other ways to disturb the peace. It's beside the point that we were trying to preserve the peace and keep millions of people from being killed. The law is the law, and breaking it makes you a criminal. Good people need to be protected from you. The fact that some of the "good" people are making weapons that can only be used to annihilate millions of innocent men, women, and children on the other side of the world is irrelevant. I do not mean to blame the police. It's not their job to sort out these questions.

My jail cell was as sparse as sparse can be. A metal slab for a bed and an open toilet. No lid on the toilet, not even a seat if I remember correctly, and no blanket for the bed. They would teach us that crime does not pay. And just to add to our lesson, there would be no food. After a while your stomach stops growling and you accept your fate. I recall having a lot of time to think that night. However, I did not have one moment's regret for the day's actions. I soon found that assuming a fetal position on the metal bed kept me from feeling the cold as much. And I remember having this feeling that I was doing one of the best things I had ever done. Even if you can't always stop evil, the very least you can do is say no to it.

Sometime the next morning we were all brought before a judge. We were charged with "resisting a police officer in the exercise of their duty" and given a date to appear in court. In order to gain our release we had to promise to stay away from Litton Industries. That was fine. The whole city now knew what was going on behind those walls, and people could find their own way of letting the company know if they did not agree.

Now it was Friday. I was not in class and I learned later that word quickly spread through the school that Mr. Small was in jail. On Monday the principal told me that I had his complete support. I heard not a word from the school board. One parent phoned to complain that a teacher had broken the law. Many others approved of what I had done. More importantly for me, students told me that they no longer wondered if I believed the things I taught them about what is moral and immoral when it comes to countries defending themselves.

Two court appearances gave me the opportunity to explain to a judge why I had taken part in civil disobedience. With a voice filled with emotion, I stated that there was no way I was willing to tell my children that our only means of defending them was by killing millions of children half a world away who were just as innocent as they were. And I quoted Einstein, who had said, "The splitting of the atom has changed everything except mankind's [*sic*] way of thinking, and thus we drift towards unparalleled disaster." Nevertheless, I was found guilty of the charge against me. At that point the prosecuting attorney jumped to his feet and recommended to the judge that I be given "an absolute discharge." The judge agreed. I said to myself, *They know we're right.*

*March 14, 1983*

# On Seeing Shannon's Pendant

What caught my eye first was its size. The silver heart that hung from a silver chain was larger than one is accustomed to seeing, and it seemed fitting that it was simply the perimeter of a heart and not a solid piece of jewelry. The next thing I noticed was that it did not hang the way these hearts usually hang. Instead, it was attached to its chain at one corner, if you can speak of a heart having a corner. So there it hung at this peculiar angle, attracting more attention than it would otherwise and making its own statement about our humanity.

Hearts can love from any position, can't they? Standing on their head, leaning to one side, or straight up; it doesn't really matter to a human heart. It's what fills in the space from top to bottom and side to side that makes the difference. Like any vessel, it's what you put into it that determines its value. Just when in our long, long history did the heart become the symbol of love? Did that awareness come from beyond us at some point? Put there perhaps by Another who knows us better than we know ourselves? In any case, we know what these hearts are for, these hearts that do more than pump blood through arteries and veins. And we know that we do them harm when we let them be filled with anything other than love. Some vessels are made to carry only the most precious of jewels.

*November 15, 2009*

# Yellow School Bus

*I* was walking along Headon Forest Drive on this third morning of March. A lovely day with those encouraging signs that winter is losing its grip on the land. The feeble grip that it had this year. One of those ubiquitous yellow school buses was approaching. The driver must have completed her morning run and was taking the empty bus home. She had stopped at the intersection and was now slowly picking up speed. Was it because she saw me looking directly at her that she decided to wave at this man she didn't even know? *That's my kind of person,* I thought to myself as I waved back. How lovely that brief moment of human contact between these two people who may never meet again.

I kept on walking, with a somewhat strange question running through me. Is it possible that on some other shore, years after we have both departed this time and place, we will meet and remember that on this morning long ago we touched each other's life? Will that kind of thing happen? I do not know the answer, but I take delight in the very question.

I hope this sister of mine found our exchange as meaningful as I did. Fellow travelers we are, whose shared greeting took hardly a second. Did she later recall the moment too? Did it make a difference in her day? How many others, here and in lands far away, shared a smile or a friendly wave of the hand with a total stranger, simply because their heart told them to? Is there another kind of global warming we do not even know about?

*March 3, 2010*

# That Train

*D*ear Derek and Celia,

A few times today I have thought of that train. You have thought of it many more times, I am sure. It is speeding its way across this beautiful and vast country we call Canada, carrying human cargo more precious to you than your own lives. With each hamlet and town it passes, each spread of lush farmland it hurtles past, each warning sound of its plaintive whistle, it grows closer and closer to its destination. And farther and farther from those it left behind. A train is an unfeeling instrument of human design, incapable of comprehending the emotions of those it bears along its predetermined path or the aching hearts of loved ones still heavy from a tearful goodbye.

You said to me this morning, Celia, "I am so sad." And I found your words so painfully understandable. Your heart must be sad too, Derek. For both of you, this is "bone of your bones and flesh of your flesh" that is being borne farther from you with each passing hour. Might it have been almost easier had Becky and Garnett hopped on a plane? Does this train create an even greater sense of the miles upon miles that will now separate you?

The roots of our joy and our sorrow seem to run equally deep. Is it because there is really only one root? Is it possible that our capacity for joy can be no greater than our ability to know sadness? Would we choose less pain if we knew it would mean less joy? The seeds of the ecstasy you will one day know when you hold Becky and Garnett's child in your arms lie side by side with the sorrow you now carry in your grieving hearts. Let your minds and your hearts go forward to that day. It is there in the tomorrows of our world. That day and this one are part of the same chain. However much we might wish it, we cannot have one without the other.

God knows how you feel now. But also how you will feel each time you see Becky again. In God your sorrow is already being turned into joy in the great, unending present where the One who made us dwells. The day of your rejoicing approaches at the same rate as that speeding train. Both are on the track we mortals call *time*.

Love and blessings,
Phil

*May 11, 2011*

# To the Edge and Back

*I*t was a Saturday afternoon in the fall of 1958. I was into my second month of teaching in a large Catholic high school in Montreal. The novelty and excitement of the change from an elementary school in Toronto had ended earlier than I thought they would. Everything familiar to me had been taken away. I gladly would have walked back to the city where I had spent four happy years. Back there was home. But that world was now closed. A state of total despondency had taken possession of me.

I lay face down on my bed. Sleep did not come, however welcome it would have been. This was not ordinary fatigue. I was tired of life, not work. It had been so easy to turn down the invitation to go for a drive to see the trees in their brilliant October colours. Who cared about beautiful trees if life had no colour?

My overly logical mind and my intense nature took over. One stark question demanded an answer: Why should I ever again get back up off this bed? It soon occurred to me that in a few hours it would be time to join the others for supper. Just as quickly, that thinking was challenged. If a hundred years from now my remains lie buried in the ground, and that's the end of me, will it matter then if I got up and nourished myself today? If it won't matter then, it doesn't matter now. Soon another thought arose. At some point this weekend I will have to mark tests and prepare lessons for my students for Monday morning. The same objection immediately knocked down that concern. If a hundred years from now both they and I are gone without a trace, will it really matter whether I made the effort to teach them well? If it won't matter then, why does it matter now? My mind went through the list but could come up with no compelling reason, none that stood the rigorous test of time, for making the effort to get up off that bed. I felt no impulse to end my life, but neither did I see any reason to extend it. What was I to do?

Yes, what was I to do? In my depressed state I coldly weighed my options. Perhaps life was totally absurd. Pointless. Devoid of any ultimate meaning. We wring whatever pleasure we can out of our time here and pass into oblivion. Should I accept that and be satisfied? Live without any answer to the why of existence? No longer bother myself with the question? As much as a part of me wished I could do that, I knew it was not an option for me. Augustine had to be right: "Whatever is not eternal is nothing." I knew I agreed with him. Not because I wanted to—I just did. But did I have proof that life has meaning? No, I didn't. So that was not a reason for getting up off my bed. Where did that leave me?

It seemed to leave me with two possibilities: I could get up and go on, but without any assurance that the effort would prove worthwhile. Or I could simply accept the hopelessness of the situation and give up. Just stay there, drift down into a total depression, and let others decide what to do with me. No more of this useless striving to make sense of it all. The painful struggle would be over.

However tempting that seemed, something deep inside forced my mind back to the first possibility. What if life did have meaning after all, even though I could not see it or feel it at the moment? Was it possible that someday I would come to believe that there is a lasting purpose to our being here? Was it worth the gamble to go on in the hope I would reach that point? Yes, I might make all this effort only to conclude that life is a fool's game, without any rhyme or reason whatsoever. But the only way I could see at that moment to remain open to the possibility of discovering that life is worthwhile—however slim that possibility—would be to keep going. How else could I hold that door open? On that October afternoon there was no other reason I could give myself for getting up off that bed. It seemed enough. Barely. So I got up.

*February 18, 2016*

# Part 2

## *Breath of Angels*

(Title of a song written by Maureen Ennis)

# Warm Wheels

"*H*ere, take this one; it has warm wheels." I turned and saw a woman lift her bag of groceries out of a shopping cart and offer the cart to another woman. They were probably both in a hurry that afternoon of the last day of the year. "Thank you and Happy New Year!" said the lady who had just entered the supermarket. As the other woman and I walked out together, I couldn't resist saying that this was the first time I had ever heard "warm wheels" used in this context. Then I added, "It probably means you have a warm heart." I fully expected that to be the end of our brief exchange, but our cars were parked quite close to one another, and so we kept chatting as we walked. What happened next is not easy to explain—and even harder to understand.

Out of what seemed like nowhere came this impulse to share with her a short piece I wrote back in May of 1994. As we stood beside her car, with a light rain beginning to fall, she listened very intently as I recited from memory what I had written several years earlier. The moment I finished she said with some insistence, "I have to have a copy of that poem!" Simone explained that her "wonderful man" was seriously ill with prostate cancer and that this piece would be meaningful to him. She gave me her e-mail address, and I promised to send her my reflection.

Later Simone would write that she told Bob she had met an angel that day. "Why else would you, out of the blue and for no reason at all, tell me this poem? It's like you *knew* about my pain and my hopes and prayers!" Her words brought me back to the events of that afternoon. I had been later than I wanted to be in leaving for the post office, and then had spent a few extra minutes in conversation with someone. The only reason I had gone into Longo's was to drop off a card to a friend who works there. Had that taken a minute more or a minute less, had I left earlier for the post office, had I not taken the time to talk with an employee there, I would not have been about to exit the supermarket just as Simone was making her "warm wheels" offer to this other woman. It struck me that each thing I had done since leaving the house that day had to have gone exactly the way it did for us to meet at that very moment. And if either of us had parked in a different area, that sharing would never have happened.

What prompted me anyway to even think of reciting this piece to her? It didn't fit in with anything either of us had said before. It certainly had nothing to do with warm wheels on a shopping cart. And yet it was just the right thing to have happen at that time between these two strangers.

Have you ever felt that you were being used—in a good way? Can you blame me for this feeling I have that we are not alone in the universe?

*January 19, 2010*

# All Those Bits of Matter

*I* kept staring at the trees and the rocks and the tall grass by the roadside as we left Peterborough behind us that morning. Something seemed very different about them this time. They were no longer totally outside of me. Totally other. We were one, they and I. I could feel it. I found myself thinking about all the bits of matter that have ever gone into the making and sustaining of what I call *my body*. And I was suddenly filled with a sweet sense of gratitude towards each one of them, however minuscule they might have been or for however long or short a period of time they were a part of me. They and I were together for some portion of my journey. They were my kin. Some of them still are. Without them I could not be.

What did those inspired faith seekers of long ago mean when they said that God took dust of the Earth and breathed life into it? Was that their version of what we now call the Big Bang? What I like to call the Big Love. Was I there in some form in that tiny fraction of a nanosecond of unbridled energy at the dawn of all that is? Or at least was the stuff of me there? The dust, or what would become dust.

But why do I keep feeling that I am more than dust? Is it that breath thing? Can matter love, all by itself? If I tell you that I love you, I so much want that to mean more than those bits of matter speaking for me. However grateful I may be to them. Could it actually be true that I am made in the image and likeness of Love? That I was created to love? And to be loved? Is that why I am happiest when I love? And when I am loved? It wasn't my idea to be like this, you know. And sometimes I almost wish I weren't this way. Whose idea was it anyway?

*June 4, 2014*

# Goodness

$G$ood morning, Dala!

Do you ever have times when you just have to write a song? When the lyrics are nipping at the heels of your mind and they just want out? Well, that's how I feel right now, except that my words don't come with a beautiful melody. I know the last thing you need is another e-mail from me, but I just can't help myself. Hope you'll excuse me on the same compassionate grounds you would extend to a fellow songwriter.

Late yesterday afternoon I was out driving around doing some errands. As is often the case, I had a Dala CD playing. Though I like to emphasize that I love you even more than your music (the artist is more important than the art), this doesn't mean that I don't adore your music. I do, and I regard it as an extension of your own hearts and souls. Because it is! It comes from deep within the two of you. I always listen so attentively to the lyrics. Words mean a great deal to me, and some of your phrases are so beautiful and so profound. In any case, there I was driving around Burlington listening to Dala, but there was something more than words and melody coming through and filling my mind and especially my heart. The only term I can use to describe it is *goodness*. The goodness of these two young women was filling the space around me. Now how can goodness come through a car's speakers, you might ask. I really don't think it can. Unless perhaps you are blessed in knowing the people behind the lovely voices and you have already been touched by their goodness. Then it can. And it did. I thank you for that. It was a lovely moment that endured long after I got home and parked the car in the garage. You came into the house with me. You even sat down to supper with me. And I talked with Margaret about you.

*Goodness* is such a simple word and one we don't hear that often. For me it is one of the most beautiful words in any language, and it is a word that can bring tears to my eyes when I recall its presence in people. It is a word that appears in a refrain on the first page of the Bible. Even God seems impressed with goodness and is, of course, its ultimate Source. A long, long time ago Saint Augustine wrote: "God does not love us because we are good, but rather we are good because God loves us." And we are at our best when we are true to that goodness. It is then that we are most ourselves. The reward is joy—a profound inner peace and harmony that shows itself in joy. I am not the only one to notice the joy that walks out onto the stage with you and is so visible in the loving friendship that is at the heart of Dala. And just like goodness, joy reminds us where it comes from. Over a hundred years ago, a very good man by the name of Léon Bloy said that joy is the infallible sign of God's presence in a person. I love that insight, put so simply and so beautifully. When we are not true to our God-given goodness, we may put on the mask of a phony joviality and pretend we have found happiness, but it will all be a facade and good people will see through it. Joy comes from the depths and cannot be hidden. It is the goodness of life asserting itself.

Keep on loving goodness and truth and beauty and your family and friends and the simple things in life. And the great gift of music you have been given.

So, dear Sheila and Amanda, I give thanks for your goodness and your joy. And I give thanks for the grace of knowing you and loving you.

Thank you for being such beautiful reflections of a Goodness that comes from far beyond any of us.

Phil

*October 31, 2007*

$D$ear God,

My friend Vanessa keeps hitting a wall. You know the kind of wall it is. She would like to see beyond that wall, to see more clearly where You would have her go. She does not know which road to take. Please help her.

After You raised your Son Jesus from the dead, walls were no obstacle to Him. Even though the disciples were in a room with all the doors closed because they were afraid, Jesus simply went right through that wall and appeared in their midst. Please have Jesus pierce this wall that blocks Vanessa's path. Let Your light shine through and show her the way.

Please give her a sense of Your presence within her as she seeks to know Your will. And give her the peace of knowing that You will always be with her on whatever road she may take. Let her see that there is nowhere she can go that You will not follow, for Your infinite love for her knows no bounds and knows no conditions. Give her a sense of the freedom of the daughters and sons of God. Take away from her any fear she may have that she might not be pleasing to You. Fear is what kept those disciples locked in that room. Jesus came through the walls of that room and the walls of their fear and brought them peace. "Peace be with you" were His first words to them. Please have Jesus do the same for my friend Vanessa.

*September 2, 2009*

# In Love with the Universe

$G$ood morning, Catherine!

I have thought of Brian Swimme's facts about the universe so often since I read your very complete notes on his talk. Each time I think about the absolute vastness of space I am left in a state of total awe. My mind grows silent and I feel as though I am on the verge of mentally passing out.

Words seem completely useless here. When I read of a hundred billion galaxies, each one containing a hundred billion stars like our sun, my mind goes blank. When we read that the Andromeda Galaxy is 2 1/2 million light years away, and that the light we now see from this galaxy left there *that long ago*, what are we supposed to do if not go into some kind of trance?

When I was twenty-five and teaching in a large high school in Montreal, I spent a whole year in a state of mental and spiritual exhaustion as I struggled with all kinds of questions. Every day was a dark and heavy day in which I tried to understand why we are here and what, if any, purpose we have. I remember at one point spending days wondering why anything at all exists. Why couldn't there simply have been nothing? If that's not a contradiction in terms. No plants, no animals, no people, no Earth, no sun, no moon, no stars, no universe, not even the chaos Genesis speaks of...*NOTHING!!!* It seemed to me that that would have been the more *normal* situation. Why things *had to be* was a gnawing question. I wanted to understand it all. And, of course, I couldn't. I sensed that even when science will have spoken its final word, my question will still be there: *Why* is there something rather than nothing? Finally, I had to accept that things *are. They simply are! ISness* surrounds us on all sides. *NOTHINGness* has never had its day. Or it still would. I had to humbly acknowledge that I wasn't going to arrive at understanding the *why* of it all. For my own sanity, I needed to start from the reality of everything that is and go on from there. The *what* of things was right there in my face, but it was humbling to have to accept that the *why* of things was so far beyond my knowing. I wanted to be the equal of whatever force put all this in motion. And if there was a Someone behind it all, why couldn't I have been that Someone? Even that brazen a question was not too much for a mind that wanted to be without limit in its understanding.

Now I simply bow before the Maker of all that is. Only God is God, and I am so profoundly grateful to have been given the immense privilege of being a tiny part of the conscious element of this whole vast creation. The fact that it is all so far beyond my comprehension no longer frustrates me; it merely fills me with awe. And sends me to my knees at times. Prayer—the kind that recognizes the difference between the Creator and the creature—seems so very appropriate. No words are necessary. Or even possible.

At other times our need to express our innermost selves in words takes over. We know that somehow words do matter and that we will always have the need to speak to ourselves and others the truths that need to be spoken. Thomas Berry is right when he says that we have to "fall in love with the universe." That's like saying that fish have to fall in love with water. What would fish do if they had a way of defending themselves against the polluting of the water that surrounds them and sustains them? What should we be doing on their behalf and on our own? The Earth can no longer be divided into "them and us"—all these "lesser creatures" and ourselves. We are one family of the living. "We live and move and have our being" in the physical world no less than the spiritual. Perhaps it is time to learn from those who inhabited this part of the Earth before us that the physical and the spiritual are not as totally distinct as we sometimes imagine.

Was there an instant in time when all that now is was present in one "place"? And did everything suddenly head off in all kinds of different directions in one Big Bang? It is fascinating to think of that possibility. This would mean that the matter that now forms my body was once present beside the star that is farthest from here in the most distant galaxy. They were there together in *that great moment*. The cosmic dust that became the fingers that move across these keys was once neighbour to solar systems light years from here. Is it all possible? Who can say that it isn't? Francis of Assisi called the sun his brother and the moon his sister. Where did he get this beautiful sense of his kinship with celestial bodies? Did the mystic in him simply recognize that we are all creatures of the one Maker? All bound together in our common origin and forever dependent on one another.

Love,
Phil

*February 1, 2014*

# The Hug

*H*e was Asian, she Caucasian. He in his mid-thirties, she in her mid-forties. He sitting at a table, she on her way out of the busy McDonald's. She noticed him first; he quickly rose to greet her. She wrapped her arms around him; he joined in the embrace. Drawing back, she stood with her hand on his shoulder. She expressed surprise at seeing him there. Hadn't they moved to another part of the city?

The Saturday morning crowd just kept on eating. I stopped, drawn instead into the warmth of the moment. All the peoples of the Earth were hugging one another and I did not want to miss the peace and the joy the vision brought me. A few seconds of simple human love. How nourishing the sight!

That coupon for a free Egg McMuffin was worth so much more than an Egg McMuffin.

*February 18, 1995*

# On Being Human

*"I* love being human," you wrote. Such simple words. Such a profound statement. That's how I feel too. Here we are poised somewhere between the animals in the fields and the angels above. Fashioned of flesh and bone and sinew like these other creatures of the Earth, yet endowed with qualities of mind and heart that point us beyond this time and place. A marriage of matter and spirit we are, of the visible and the invisible. "Called," as I once wrote, "to know and to know that I know ... to love and to know that I love." Given the awesome power to choose between what is good and what is evil, between what makes us more truly human and what makes us less than we are meant to be. A power so great that we often flee from the nobility to which it calls us.

And then there is the whole universe of our feelings. These "beautiful, painful, glorious" feelings, as you so aptly described them. They can transport us to moments of intense happiness and joy or plunge us to depths of sadness and despair we fear we may never escape. Though they are not always of our choosing, they are born of our humanity, and how we respond to them determines how true to ourselves we will be. We can pretend they are not ours, we can do our best not to feel what we are feeling, but our flight from them will always be a flight from ourselves. It is only in taking ownership of them that we will ever find our way home to our own heart and our own soul. At times we will be able to say a full yes to where they would lead us; on other occasions we will need to say no to where they would have us go. But feel them we must if we are to be fully human.

It is these painful, glorious feelings that cause our hearts to ache for a fallen member of our race we do not even know, or burst with pride over the accomplishments of a child, or melt with tenderness at the sight of a face we love. They are our friends, and without them we cannot be ourselves. Unfeeling, coldly rational beings, computers on two legs, would never be able to give our world the warmth of human affection and caring we all crave. I am glad that you love being human.

*December 16, 2008*

# Prayer for Jessica

$D$ear God, I want to pray this morning for my friend Jessica. Please guide my mind and my heart so that I may ask for those things You would have me pray for.

Please give your daughter Jessica a deep sense of Your comforting Presence through all her days and her nights. Grant her the grace of falling asleep at the close of each day aware that Your gaze is fixed on her as Your beloved daughter "in whom You are well pleased." And help her to wake gently from sleep each morning with the carefree heart of a daughter of the King, filled with the confidence that Your love goes with her at each step she takes. Give her the heart of your friend Mary, who understood that You took more delight in the simple pleasure of her company than in anything she did for You. Grant Jessica the grace to see what matters most to You and what matters least, what furthers Your kingdom here on Earth and what does not. When to say yes and when to say no.

Please help her to see herself as Your little child, her Daddy's girl. Give her the knowledge that the great tenderness she feels for her children is a mere reflection of the tenderness You feel for her. That You care far more for the love in her heart than the work of her hands. That her only call is to be Jessica, no one else. That You love her as much when she is at play as when she is "about [her] Father's business." That doing fewer things with a peaceful heart is better than doing many things with anxious striving.

*March 13, 2014*

# Candles

*D*ear Maureen and Karen and Teresa,

I can't tell you how much Margaret and I enjoyed your Christmas show the other night. The audience was so totally into it. You must have found it easy to feed off that crowd.

You have probably heard the saying that it is better to light a candle than to curse the darkness. God knows there is more than enough darkness in our world these days. You alluded to that the other evening, Maureen. Several times yesterday I thought of how the Ennis Sisters are going around the country lighting candles. These are not candles that are placed on a candlestick. They are the candles that the three of you, with the wonderful contributions of Mark and Matthew, light in the hearts and minds of all those who attend your concerts. These candles are not visible in the ordinary way, but they are visible. I could see them on the faces of those who walked beside us as we left the theatre. You sang of the joy of this wonderful season of the year and you projected the joy that is there in your own hearts and souls. "The medium is the message," as McLuhan said, and you were such a beautiful medium of the message you brought. You lit candles, candles that were not extinguished as people walked out into the biting wind of a cold winter night.

Keep on doing what you are doing. You are making a difference in our world, and that matters. People are happier after one of your shows, and happy people are more loving people. You touch more than those who are "the fortunate ones" you sing and recite and dance for. Those people leave and spread the joy that is in their own hearts. Because joy can never be kept just for ourselves. By its very nature it spills over onto others. Those ripples begin with you. Your love travels beyond the walls of the venues your voices fill. How wonderful.

Just had to share these thoughts with you. They come from a heart that still feels the warmth of the candle you lit inside me.

With my love and admiration,
Phil

*December 16, 2016*

# Chocolate Chip Cookies

$M$y friend wrote that she is making chocolate chip cookies for her neighbours. She admits that she may keep some for herself, but there will definitely be cookies taken to those who live near her. What a great way to meet and become friends with these other folk who live in this little corner of Nova Scotia that she and her husband moved into not all that long ago.

How will Meaghan feel as she bakes these little gifts for the people who will now be the faces she sees as she goes to and fro in her new neighbourhood? What impulse even led her to think of doing this? And how many people around the world will open their door today to the smiling face of someone who just happened to bring them a little present, simply because they felt like doing it?

What is it about us humans that impels us to do these things? From what hidden stream do these stirrings of tenderness and love arise? Are we really made in the image and likeness of Love, and are we most in harmony with something deep within us when we act in this way? Do we feel good about ourselves in these moments because we have come forth from Goodness? Just wondering. I am always trying to figure out where things come from. I can't help it. And don't even want to.

*June 25, 2009*

# Fabian

*(a close friend who journeyed bravely through Parkinson's)*

$D$ear Fabe,

It's one year ago today since you left us. We want you to know that we miss you. And that we always will.

I had a dream the other day, Fabe. It was one of those kinds of dreams where you aren't sure if you are more asleep than awake or more awake than asleep. But I have to tell you about it. First, however, we need to go back to the day when Margaret and I were visiting you and Myrna and I asked what you thought about during those quiet times when you were just sitting there by yourself in your chair. You replied in one word: "God." Well, here's what happened in my strange dream.

In my dream Jesus did not die at age thirty-three. Instead, he lived to be an old man, but was still the same Jesus who came down from heaven to live among us and show us how to love. The Father had decided that we needed to have his Son stay with us for the whole of a normal life, then get sick and die the way all of us do as we age. So in my dream I was visiting Jesus when he was old and sick. He did not have much energy and was finding it difficult to talk for very long. So I just sat there with him to keep him company. Sometimes I would stare at him and wonder what he was thinking. After a long time with the two of us sitting there in silence, I said, "Jesus, what do you think about when you are sitting there?" He waited for a few moments and then in a quiet voice said, "Fabian."

Just thought I should tell you about my dream.

Your friend,
Phil

*May 9, 2017*

# Part 3

*Conception and Birth*

# Such Wonderful News

*D*ear Theresa and David,

Margaret and I want to thank you for sharing such wonderful news with us on Sunday. We are so very happy for you. And for this tiny, precious life that has so freshly arrived on the human scene. Welcome, little one!

Years ago Margaret and I attended a pro-life evening in Ottawa. I still remember walking into that auditorium and seeing the three or four desks that were set up on the stage waiting to be occupied. One of them had the name Dr. Jefferson on it. This was a long time ago, as I said, and I still carried certain stereotypes of doctors in my male mind. Two of them were shattered at once when an African-American woman walked out onstage to sit at that desk. She brought with her the eloquence of a Martin Luther King Jr., and used it to great effect. All through her speech, each time she referred to the unborn, she called them "these youngest of our kind." There is such beauty in that phrase, and such power. A beauty and a power that come from a true naming of this reality. And now, Theresa, you are privileged to carry one of "these youngest of our kind" so close to your loving heart.

Just recently a friend of ours sent us a piece in which he quoted a brief statement of Saint Augustine's that I had not come across before: "*Volo ut sis.*" ("I want you to be.") Our friend said that this is the simplest description of love that he knows. It is certainly a profound affirmation of the very being of another. And this is exactly what the two of you have said to this tiny life you have called into existence. And it is what God says to each one of us He calls from nothingness into life: *I want you to be.* Another of Augustine's sayings, and one of my favourites, is "O God, use me." Isn't it totally beyond our imagining to be used by God in the way in which you have so recently been used? The longings of your hearts for this precious young life were more powerful than whatever other prayers you may have said. And now they have been answered.

The smile on your face the other day said it all, Theresa. It made me think of that beautiful saying of Léon Bloy, "Joy is the infallible sign of God's presence in a person." Your joy was the unmistakable sign of the miracle growing inside you. That, too, is God's presence.

I send my love to this "youngest of our kind." And to the two of you.

Phil

*February 15, 2011*

# She's Gone

$D$ear Mary,

Thank you for your e-mail message this morning. I didn't really have to open it. "She's gone" said it all. Though on one level this news was no surprise, on another level it still came as a shock. As I left your mother's room yesterday afternoon, I doubted that I would ever see her alive again. And yet reading your words on that screen, confirming what I sensed would probably happen at any moment, still seemed in some way unreal. How could this person who had smiled at me less than twenty-four hours ago now be gone? It's the finality of death that makes it so difficult to grasp. There is no contrast anywhere like the one between the living and the dead.

It was only as I drove away from the hospital that the complete picture of what was going on in that room started to come into focus for me. I don't know if I can find the words to adequately describe the scene. On a bed a woman lay dying, already into the countdown of the last few hours of her life. Only a few feet away another woman was nourishing from her own body a brand new life that had come into our world just weeks before. The one who lay dying had years earlier held this other woman to her breast, had looked down in wonder and amazement at the tiny new life she too fed from her body. All these years later death and new life were here side by side. Sad as it was, there was something so very fitting about it all. The starkness of the contrast spoke so clearly of the triumphant march of life. Death cannot halt it. As long as there is a mother to nurse her young, the human story will keep right on going.

I have always been somewhat in awe at the sight of a woman breastfeeding her baby. Margaret never seemed more mother than when she had one of our children at her breast. We men know nothing of this. Though the child is ours as well, we have not carried her for the better part of a year inside our very body, nor can we nourish her out of our own substance. There must be times when it all seems anything but a miracle—in the middle of the night, for example. Nevertheless, I cannot imagine women not having moments when they are overwhelmed by the mystery and the sheer beauty of this gift they have been given. On the surface the scene in that hospital room seemed so ordinary. What was really going on was anything but.

Some aspects of your thirtieth birthday may seem surreal. One might even hesitate to use the word *celebrate* this year. And yet the handing on and the nourishing of life are truly worthy of that word. I have no doubt whatsoever that thirty years ago your mother considered you an extraordinarily beautiful birthday gift. This year Kiera Kathleen was the gift your mum received as she moved towards another kind of birthday, a birth into life without end.

Lovingly,
Phil

*September 29, 2005*

# How Could It Be

*D*ear Angela,

What a shock it must have been! One that shook you to the very bottom of your soul. For as long as you had lived, a full half-century of life, you had known where you came from—from the same two people as your brothers. This was as true as your own existence. No wonder the words that fell from your aunt's mouth were more than you could take in. How could it be? How could it be? Your mother and father were not really your mother and father. It was almost as though you had been told you didn't exist. Another woman had carried you in her womb—and had then given you away. How could that be possible? How could a woman part with her own flesh and blood? "Was I not worth keeping? I might as well have been told that I was soon going to die, that my life was over. That is how it seemed. I was not who I thought I was. The cold reality of it all was more than I could bear."

You must wonder now, Angela, how you ever survived that time. You know that it took all the love your husband and children could pour into you to get you through those awful days and nights. They did not care whose womb you had come from. They simply saw the beauty of who you are and loved you all the more. That love, plus the merciful grace of God our Father and the help of Our Blessed Mother, kept you going through those dark days that stretched into months and even years. Your waking moments were filled with tears and endless prayers. Deep emotional pain was your constant companion. You wondered if life would ever be the same again.

Ever so slowly, almost without your being aware of it, from the depths of your own maternal heart a realization began to grow. Was it perhaps love, a love so great that it put your welfare before her deep longing to keep you, that made it possible for the one who bore you to let you go? Could it be that the heart of a mother can allow itself to be broken into a thousand pieces if this is what she knows is best for her child? Did she cry herself to sleep at night as she prayed for the baby she could no longer hold in her arms? Have her prayers been following you all these years, bringing down blessings on you and those you love?

We read in Scripture that "eye has not seen nor ear heard nor has it entered into the human heart what things God has in store for those who love Him." God knows, Angela, how great is your love for Him. Would it be too much to hope that one day in heaven three women will meet? You and Elizabeth and the other mother you have never met. Will you be embraced by two who have loved you all your life? The one who welcomed you into her heart and her home, and the one in whose womb God knit together your tiny body. They say that with God all things are possible. What a beautiful dream to carry with you through this second half of your life!

For now, let your days be filled with the joy you and James share in watching your lovely family find their way in life. Draw deep nourishment for your own soul from your awareness that they would not be had a woman not loaned God her body so that you might "have life and have it to the full."

With my love and admiration,
Phil

*Thanksgiving Day, 2008*

# The First Day of November

*H*appy anniversary, Angela! This is an anniversary you may not be thinking of, but in some ways it is the most significant of all your anniversaries. This is the anniversary of the day you were conceived. Without this one, there would be no others.

A number of years ago I found myself wondering why we do not celebrate this very first moment of our existence. After all, we have the Feast of the Annunciation on March 25, nine months before Jesus' birth. We are commemorating Mary's consent to be the mother of Jesus and, therefore, commemorating as well the day that Jesus was conceived. Why not remember in a special way this most significant moment in our own journey? The day God first called us into existence. It does not matter that we do not know the exact day. Neither does the Church know the exact date of Jesus' conception. Knowing the very day isn't what matters. Being filled with wonder and awe and deep gratitude is what counts.

And so, Angela, I want to tell you how grateful I am that around this time of year you took your first step onto the human scene. It was at once both the tiniest step you ever took and also the biggest one. All the others you would ever take depended on this one. A man and a woman made love and you came to be. You came to be because God was also making love at that moment. God was calling your name, calling you into life. The same God who at the dawn of creation said, "Let there be light" was now saying, "Let there be Angela. I want her to come to know me and to know how much I love her. She will be my beautiful daughter."

Margaret and I rejoice with you on this first day of November. What a wonderful way to begin this new month! With a prayer of gratitude to God that on this day many years ago our friend Angela was given the precious gift of life. It is our great privilege to know you and to love you.

Phil

*November 1, 2010*

# A Reluctant Yes

*H*e knew he was not ready to be a father. This was not supposed to be happening. Nevertheless, here he was watching the birth of his first child, the child who was arriving a few years before he had intended to cross the threshold into becoming a parent. Life was now beyond his control.

The birth canal was more than a passageway between a womb and the outside world. It was a fork in the road that led to a life of new responsibilities and unforeseen challenges. Things would never be the same again. He knew that, and a part of him still wished he could go back to the way things had been before.

Then suddenly everything changed. There she was! *She* was ready, however unprepared mother and father might be. Both would take her in their arms and know the ecstasy of feelings they had never experienced before. This was a life that only the two of them could have called into being. One was now mother. One was now father. Wherever the road ahead might lead, they would forever be Quinn's parents.

He would later say that if anything were to happen to him now, he would not be leaving here without a trace. Quinn would be his ongoing presence in the world, and her children and her children's children would carry elements of his seed for long generations to come.

And here and now she would bring a purpose and joy to his days that no one else could have given him. His reluctant yes would grow into such deep gratitude that she had surprised him on life's way.

*August 1, 2016*

# Conceived Twice

*D*ear Kristal and Bryan,

Some children are conceived twice. Once inside the body of their birth mother and then again inside the heart and soul of the woman who receives this child from God as her own. And they are fathered twice. The second fathering is into the strong arms of the man who will forever be there to protect and guide. This child is truly theirs. He has grown inside the womb of their deep longing to one day look on his face and tell him how much they love him.

From this day on, your home is Bradley's home. This is now where he belongs. This is where he will learn to say Mom and Dad. This is where he will grow into the young man he will one day become. You are family. The arms that hugged each other have opened wide to take into their embrace a precious young life sent by God in answer to fervent prayer.

At church on Sunday I saw a young boy with *FIRST ROUND DRAFT PICK* on his sweatshirt. A few hours later I stood on the street holding the sign *ADOPTION: THE LOVING OPTION*. As I stood there, I found myself thinking that Bradley should have a shirt with the words *NUMBER ONE DRAFT PICK*. He is certainly number one in *your* hearts. And in the hearts of all those who form the warm, loving circle of your family and friends. He will never lack for love.

Margaret and I join so many others in sending you our warmest congratulations as you officially welcome Bradley into your home. He has had a home in your hearts ever since you first knew how deeply you longed for his presence in your lives. How truly fitting that he will be there at your table at this time we call Thanksgiving. God is good.

With our love and prayers,
Phil and Margaret

*October 6, 2011*

# Ender

$D$ear Jermanda,

Margaret and I thank you for our first visit with Ender. It was so special to look with love on his tiny face and to hold his delicate body in our arms. There is nothing delicate about that cry, however. He will make sure no one fails to acknowledge that he is here.

As we drove away from that first encounter with this new citizen of our world, I kept thinking how only the two of you—no others—could have passed on to him the incredible gift of life. His only chance at existence depended entirely on you two making the decision to invite him into the human family. Because your paths one day crossed and you chose to merge your separate journeys into one, Ender is now here among us. Each of you gave of your very substance so that he might one day share in the immense joy of knowing and being known, of loving and being loved. He will always be the visible expression of the love that drew you to each other. He is as truly Jermanda as you are.

In time he will move from the nourishment he draws from his mother's breast to take his place around the family table. A table fashioned from the wood of a barn that once sheltered animals who gave of their substance that we might live, just as the tree had given of its substance. And on it goes. Life supporting life in its relentless upward spiral, all of us bound together in this mysterious and sacred web that has brought you to Ender.

All my love,
Phil

*April 23, 2014*

# First Letting Go

$M$y friend Paula has begun to wean Nateo, and she is finding this emotionally difficult. She will be returning to work soon and, though she will be able to continue nursing him at night, she knows that this is the beginning of the end of that uniquely intimate mother-child relationship that only a woman fully understands. At some level Paula must sense that this is but the first of many times when she will have to let go of what her mother's heart would love to hold on to just a little longer.

And yet she knows too that it will always be love that will call her to graciously accept each letting go. A love that never ceases to choose what is best for this child of her womb, this flesh of her flesh. If only this love could take away the pain that goes with each new step of his journey to a separate existence. Gabriel Marcel had the insight to state, "Love is the meeting of two freedoms," and in some way this meeting of two freedoms seems to be there even from the moment of birth. As close as they may then be, as close as they may always remain, one will never be the other. The infant who longs for the comfort of his mother's breast must one day learn that he cannot remain there forever, and the mother who longs to hold him there forever must accept that this cannot be.

And yet she will always know that his first home was in the warm confines of her welcoming body, and the first milk that nourished him was her very own. He, too, will always know this. They will forever be mother and son.

*March 24, 2010*

# A Mother's Love

*O*ur daughter Michelle wrote to a friend: "Uncovering the depths of a mother's love is quite life-changing and awe-inspiring, and that love will be the basis upon which you parent her forever." While reading those lines, I had the impression that Michelle was surprised to discover just how deep and how vast were her own maternal instincts and emotions.

What caught my attention was the extent to which she saw herself in some way as a spectator in the face of the changes that transpired within her on becoming a mother. She did not know that she could love this much.

Where did that love come from? Was she touched by a power that came from beyond her? Was Kazantzakis right when he spoke of a "gigantic breath" that blows through heaven and earth and "in our hearts and the heart of every living thing"? How else could Michelle be in awe over the depth of her love for her own child? Perhaps she is not the only mother of her child. Is she the good soil on which the seed of another Love was sown?

Michelle has clearly spoken her yes to a Love that has changed her forever and left her in awe. One more reminder that we dwell in mystery.

*July 31, 2016*

*Happy Birthing Day to you*
*Happy Birthing Day to you*
*Happy Birthing Day, dear Catherine*
*Happy Birthing Day to you.*

Good morning, Catherine!

It would be natural to have your mind go back at some point to twenty-six years ago this day. The day when your body decided it was time to send Amanda out into the world to begin life on her own. It must be ever so special to realize that you were the sacred vessel in which God knit together her tiny body. Those little arms and legs, those delicate fingers and toes, those ears and eyes and nose and mouth. That beating heart. All of that took place so close to your own heart. Its steady rhythm would have been the first sounds her newly formed ears ever heard and the comforting lullaby she first fell asleep to. Amanda mentioned the song "Miracle of Miracles" at one point during dinner last night. How very appropriate those words. Had she been able to, she would have sung them in the womb.

This is the day we sing the praises of love. I know two people who have more reason than most to cherish this day. One is a mother and one is a daughter. The love between them is so beautiful to see. Wherever that daughter goes, whatever lives she touches, the mother will be there too and she will touch those lives as well. Her heart must come close to being overwhelmed at times. One can take only so much joy.

Just had to write this for you today.

Love,
Phil

*February 14, 2008*
*Valentine's Day*

# Part 4

*Love and Marriage*

# For Margaret

You came unbidden into my life. I didn't know I was looking for you. Though I was. You didn't know you were looking for me. Though you were. Our paths were already set. Or so we thought. On a beautiful July day in 1968 those paths crossed. It was a long time before I realized the full import of that moment. Ever so gradually things came into focus for me, and I came to know myself in the grace of meeting you. All along I had been scanning the crowd of each group I met, searching for a certain face. Though I could never admit to myself what I was doing. Every once in a while I would think I had found the face I didn't even know I was looking for. Then at some level deeper than conscious thought I would say to myself, *No, that's not the one.* And then I met you.

I dared not let myself even imagine what this meeting could mean. However, my heart knew in an instant that my search was over. The search I could never acknowledge I was engaged in had come to an end. The face in the crowd I had longed to find was now before me. It was such a beautiful face. But there was more than ordinary beauty here; there was such peace and gentleness and love. A beautiful soul shone through. Beauty and simple goodness all wrapped in one— my heart didn't have a chance. Hearts are made for goodness; that is where they find their home. I knew where I belonged.

I am so grateful that you said yes to spending your life with me and being the beautiful face I wake up to each day. I thank God for the gift of you.

With all my love,
Phil

*May 24, 2008*

*D*ear Rebecca and Garnett,

It was with great joy that I learned of your engagement. It is always special to see that two people have found each other and have come to know that they belong together—that they are called to share the journey back to God. How marvelous beyond words!

I offered a prayer of thanksgiving this morning for the gift of your love. Your one love. I like to reflect at times on this beautiful mystery: Two people meet and get to know each other and "fall in love," as we say. Then after a certain period of time, they find themselves instinctively using the phrase "our love." Not my love for you and your love for me, but our love. They don't decide to do this. It just happens. As though they had been given some secret knowledge that came from beyond themselves that when two people reach a certain depth in their love, their separate loves meet somewhere between them, join, and become one entity. They are now two persons and their one love. A trinity. It seems to me that when two people genuinely love each other, they become a reflection of what goes on within God where the Spirit *is* the very love between the other two Persons. Their one Love. God is the Source of all love, and I see God present in a special way when two people come to know that the bond between them is no longer the separate attractions that drew them to each other, but this one mysterious reality they now call "our love."

I feel a desire to say to your love: "Welcome to our world. A short while ago you did not exist, and now here you are making of our Earth a more loving, a more joyful, and a more beautiful place. We feel the warmth of your presence in our midst, and we give thanks to God for the gift that you are to all of us."

*September 11, 2010*

# One Line

*D*ear Erin and Christopher,

How truly lovely when a happy hour turns into a happy life! Did either of you have any idea when you went to that church happy hour a few years ago that you were about to meet the person you would decide to spend your life with? It would seem not if one were to judge by the winding and separate paths you each walked during the next period of your lives. True, that happy hour was followed by your first date, but it seems as though you both came away thinking that might also be your last date. And it certainly was for quite some time.

I wish I knew who first said that God writes straight with crooked lines. It had to be a very wise person. In the years before that happy hour, and in the years immediately after, you both gave God lots of crooked lines to work with. However, God could already see how straight those lines would turn out to be. Helen Keller, with her great sensitivity, once said, "I felt that there were invisible lines stretched between my spirit... and the spirits of others." Perhaps, Erin and Chris, you can see now, or at least suspect, that invisible lines had begun to form between your two spirits back then, lines that would in time bring you back home to each other. It seems, Chris, that the date that seemed to go nowhere did not leave you nowhere. It left you with the memory of a beautiful woman who still pulled at your heart on each occasion you happened to see her—even at a distance.

This gnawing memory inside you had to have an echo in Erin's heart, or we would not be here today. If you had been looking for a face in the crowd, a face you wanted to wake up to each day, so had Erin. And you both needed to see that face again to realize that it was the one you had been looking for all along. You had to come back together to see how beautifully straight God had written with all those crooked lines of your separate paths. Now you knew that there was meant to be just one path, one line. Walked together the rest of the way.

With my love and prayers,
Phil

*October 24, 2015*

# Max and Bertha

*I* had met them for the first time only a few days before. Now here they were again, out on their bicycles for a little morning exercise on this lovely fall day. We chatted briefly as they waited for the light to change. Then she headed off across the intersection. He delayed for a few moments—he had something to tell me. Did I know that she was going to be eighty on the seventh of December? The pride in his voice was unmistakable. And so beautifully touching. She was still the bride of his youth, the companion of his younger years.

However much time might have taken its toll in other ways, it had been powerless to diminish the love that would forever bind them one to the other. The young man inside still felt the need to boast of the beautiful maiden whose heart he had won. Age could not rob him of that. Before long—did he already sense it?—he would steal away in the night and she would be left behind. Should he shout out to everyone while he still could that she was his Bertha and he was so proud of her? Surely there was no need to. How could they not see?

*February 19, 1995*

Two shall be born the whole wide
world apart...and these over
unknown seas to unknown lands
shall...bend each wandering step
to this one end,
that one day out of darkness
they shall meet
and read life's meaning
in each other's eyes.[5]

*Life's meaning.* Could any two words go more directly to the heart of it all? I suspect that Susan Marr Spalding, the author of this piece, would agree with another poet, E. E. Cummings, who wrote, "Unless you love someone, nothing else makes sense." There it is! We are made to love and to be loved. When we look into the eyes of someone we love and see love looking back at us, it all comes together. There is no arguing with that experience. Love tells us more than anything else that we are at home in this vast universe. That we belong.

A wedding is the day when one says to the world: "I have found the friend I want to spend my life with. Of all the persons I have met on my journey, this is the one I want by my side for as long as I live. This is where my heart has found a home. This is where I want to stay." The vows that Jerome and Amanda make to one another today are not new. They have lived unspoken in the silence of their hearts for some time now.

It is from these silent depths that much of what is good and beautiful springs forth, often to our own amazement. We humans dwell in mystery. It is there in the background of our lives, whether we are aware of it or not. Poets and lovers know this better than anyone. However long or however intimately we may live with another, we never arrive at a point where this other can no longer surprise us in some way. Each of us is an entire universe waiting to be discovered,

---

5  Susan Marr Spalding, "Fate" (PoetryExplorer.net).

and we forever remain somewhat of a mystery even to ourselves. Gabriel Marcel, who wrote, "Love is the meeting of two freedoms," could just as truthfully have said, "Love is the meeting of two mysteries." It takes a lifetime, and then some, to fathom the beauty and the depth of this other freedom, this other mystery. This other half of my soul.

*July 2, 2011*

# La Conversation

*D*ear Jerome and Amanda,

Years ago I heard a talk on marriage given by a man from France. One of his statements has stayed with me to this day: *"Le mariage, c'est une conversation permanente."* "Marriage is a lifelong conversation" is how I like to translate that sentence. There was a moment somewhere in time when the two of you exchanged the first words that ever passed between you. There will come another moment in time when one of you will say a final farewell in the arms of the other. Between these two moments on your journey, millions of words will cross the divide that makes of each of you a separate person. Some words will seem so ordinary, on the surface of no great consequence at all. Others will be the expression of a joy too great for even the most eloquent of words, while still others may be spoken through tears that will say more than any attempt at speech. Some will be tender words, spoken in moments of special closeness; some may be words of impatience or disappointment. A few may even be spoken in anger. They will all, however, be your words, the ones that pass between just the two of you as you make your way along the path that is uniquely yours to walk. Your *conversation permanente.*

Most of these words will be spoken in the actual presence of the other. Some will be spoken in real time over a phone, others left as a voice mail. There will be those that are scribbled on a scrap of paper and left as a note when the other is still asleep. Some will be as mundane as a shopping list, while others will carry words of affection across great distances as a reminder that love is never far away. Some will be written on special stationery; others will be read off a screen. It will not matter how they arrive; it will only matter that they do, for they will be the bridge that turns your two solitudes into one love. They will be your words, owned by both of you, the raw everyday stuff of the I-Thou relationship that we call marriage. Like all things in this mysterious and wonder-filled world of ours, your words will not be without number. Though they may be in the millions, they will still be countable. One was your first. One will be your last. This makes each one so very, very precious. Nevertheless, spend them extravagantly, without even thinking of how many you may have used up. They are the gold of your existence and you are rich beyond measure.

*Bon voyage dans votre vie de couple et bonne et longue conversation!*

All my love,
Phil

*August 24, 2011*

# Hanna and Paul

We have all heard the expression "Today is the first day of the rest of your life." It would be difficult to think of an occasion more suited to that statement than one's wedding day. This is the day when two people say to each other, "However many more years I may live, I want to spend each one of them with you. You are the one I want to be with for the rest of my life. That is how much I love you." What more can one human being say to another?

What does it mean to say "I love you" in such a total way? How can I be sure that my love will last? How do I know that I will always feel this way? Erich Fromm, in his classic, *The Art Of Loving*, states: "To love somebody is not just a strong feeling—it is a decision, it is a judgment, it is a promise." And so we are here today to celebrate not only the beautiful emotional bond between the two of you but also the very conscious decision, judgment, promise you are making. You are saying, "I will always choose you, no matter what. I am giving myself to you forever." As Emily Dickinson has said, "Forever is composed of nows." It is the now of this sacred moment when you exchange your marriage vows and it is the now of all the moments of your lives from here on. In this context *forever* is such a beautiful and powerful word—a word that takes its meaning from the strong feelings of the heart and the strong commitment of the will.

So what exactly is the gift you give to each other today? Lisa Oz just this year published an excellent book entitled *US*. It's all about our relationships. Her first chapter has only one word as its title, *You*. As she says, "... all of your relationships have one thing in common: you."[6] What you give to each other today is *you*. Your own selves. You cannot give more and you should not give less. Unlike other presents, however, this one cannot be handed to the other and then forgotten. It will always be up to each of you to continue to give meaning and value to your gift: the unique and irreplaceable gift of you.

So today a gift is given and a gift is received. And your love sets out on a journey. A wise and holy man who lived a long time ago once said: "Perfect love exists between two people only when each addresses the other with the words 'O myself!'" As everyone here

6   Lisa Oz, *US* (New York: Simon and Schuster, 2010), p. 7.

knows, it takes a lifetime, and then some, to arrive at that point. It is helpful, however, to be aware from the very beginning that that is where we want our love to take us.

The prayers and best wishes of all of us go with you on your journey.

*October 24, 2010*

# Of Light and Goodness

$G$ood morning, Vanessa!

It's a little after seven. There is a red glow in the sky on one side of our house. The sun is on its way up. On the other side of our house we can see the full moon, still bright as can be in the cloudless sky. This brings to mind a thought I had a few days ago. It was just after Ray called you as you were dropping me off at our place.

I know how much you love God and how special your love for Ray has become. I got to thinking. When a person loves the light of the moon, she is also loving the sun, the source of that light. When you love the goodness you see in Ray, you are also loving the Source of that goodness. There are times when we are loving God unawares.

This in no way diminishes the beauty of our human loves. We take nothing away from the sun when we delight in the brightness of the moon. Nor do we love God less when our hearts are drawn to the goodness we see in another. It is God who made us this way. We speak of the light of the moon as though it comes from the moon. In a way it does. And we speak in the same manner of the goodness of someone we love. And well we should, with even more reason. For unlike the moon, we have to say yes to the light and goodness God pours into our hearts. Ray is good because God is good and Ray is good because Ray is good. Both are true. Like Mary, we have to say yes to God being born in us, yes to the light and goodness in our own hearts.

Delight in your love for Ray. And give thanks.

I send my love to both of you,
Phil

*December 11, 2011 (Gaudete Sunday)*

"Now taste the wine. It's very good, very dry."
Oh no, it's not, my dear. When you said, "I love you,"
I tasted but the sweetest wine.
(Lois Wyse, *Love Poems for the Very Married*)[7]

*D*ear Chris and Erin,

It may not have been at the church happy hour, the day you first met, that the conversation went like this, but it's somehow easy to imagine that words close to these could pass between the two of you now. We know you love to share a glass of wine together. And we know that you love each other. That's all this kind of exchange requires.

Those cute save-the-date coasters you sent out a few months ago did advertise *Free Drinks*. You knew how to get us here. You also knew, I'm sure, that we wouldn't be coming just for the free drinks. It would be the sweet wine of your love that we wanted to taste for ourselves.

How fitting to have wine be one of the themes of your wedding. Was it not at a wedding feast that Jesus changed water into wine so that all who were there could continue to celebrate with the bride and groom? And doesn't Jesus continue to change water into wine for couples who invite Him to join their shared journey? Would you not agree, Erin and Chris, that He has been with you from the beginning, changing the water of your first tentative attraction to each other into the full-bodied wine of the love you now share? And this fine wine will only get better with age.

We all thank you for the privilege of being here with you to taste the sweet wine of your love. That is the best free drink of all. And we wish you many, many years of sharing a glass together as you close out the day with a prayer of thanks to the God who has blessed you so abundantly.

*October 23, 2015*

---

7   Lois Wyse, *Love Poems for the Very Married* (Cleveland OH: The World Publishing Company, 1967), p. 15.

# A Lesson Learned

$W$e were poor. Very poor. And my father could find no work in our small hometown of Pembroke that winter. He would have to leave town for several months and go to work in the bush. Why he always took his carpenter's tools I'm not sure.

This was the day he would leave. His suitcase and tool kit (it looked like a second suitcase) were ready by the door. What a bad time for him to get into an argument with our mother! However, it wasn't at all unusual for them to have a disagreement over money. We were always short, and somehow my father could not help but feel that my mother didn't handle well the little he did bring home. This particular argument grew worse than the others. Perhaps my dad felt bad about having to leave home. Perhaps he worried that the money he would send back wouldn't be enough. Harsh words were exchanged. My mother was taking it pretty hard. It must have seemed so unfair to her to be blamed for their financial difficulties. There were very few jobs outside the home for women in those early days of World War II and, besides, she couldn't leave three small children alone. She sat down in a chair by the window and retreated into sullen silence. If he was going to make it all her fault, then saying nothing more was the best way to handle the situation. Let him rant on to himself.

What should he do now? It was time to leave and they weren't even talking to each other. He walked towards the door, then turned and said goodbye to his three frightened children. Then he just stood there. What was going through his mind? Should he simply walk out and leave her there to sort out her emotions after he left? Maybe this would teach her a lesson and she would realize that she should be more careful in the way she spent their money. He certainly wasn't feeling very affectionate at that moment. And she was making no move to get out of her chair and give him a hug and a kiss before he left for the winter. It was sad that he had to leave us, and this was making the whole thing even sadder.

He picked up his suitcase and was reaching for his tool kit. No, he couldn't just leave like that. He put his suitcase back down. He went over to my mother, who still sat there in the chair by the window. She was too hurt to even turn towards him, so he leaned over and kissed her on the cheek. And then he was gone.

It was many years later that the memory of that moment came back full force into my consciousness. I had no idea that it was still there. When it did return, it brought with it a clear awareness of its deep significance. In one gesture my father had reassured me that, despite the appearances of this sad time, all would be well. He would return one day and we would be family again. My father still loved my mother. I was secure. Long before I would ever see on a poster the words "Love is a decision," my father had taught me that our feelings cannot always be counted on to be the sole determinant of what is the loving thing to do.

*April 24, 2008*

# Part 5

*Hints of (Im)mortality*

*I*'ve had this awareness for a few years now that I am like a ship on the ocean that has been travelling along on one course for a long time but has suddenly made a sharp change in direction. It may still be a fair distance to land, but I have now set sail for the home port. It is off somewhere over the horizon. I cannot see it, but the water rushing by tells me that sooner or later I will get there.

This awareness provides me with a different context for the Lord's Prayer at this time in my life. I may have quite a number of years to go yet (two of my uncles lived into their mid-nineties), but my needs and my sense of what nourishes me are not what they used to be. To ask for daily bread now does not have the same meaning as it did years ago. The type of hunger I experience has undergone considerable change.

A desire for a more contemplative, more prayerful, and more reflective lifestyle has been growing in me for some time. There is a yearning for more time to pray, to visit a friend or someone in need, to read books that are good for the soul, to enjoy the peace and quiet of a walk in the woods or by the lake where God seems present in a special way. My daily bread is of a different type. I need, for now at least, to be less busy and more in tune with the particular life rhythms that come with this stage of my existence. This is what seems to feed me now. It is where I draw my strength.

The danger I face is that of not listening to the inner voice that calls me in this new direction. It is not easy to break old habits, to overcome the feeling that I need to be "doing something productive" at each moment of the day. My prayer for daily bread must be a prayer for the wisdom to let go of former ways of defining myself and for the gentle acceptance that it is all right to just be still at times and know that God is God (see Psalm 46:10).

*December 2, 2002*

# Milan's Gift

$M$y dear Milan,

One month ago today, Margaret and I had the privilege of taking you and Ellen and your son for a sail on Lake Ontario. Just two days ago, many of your family members and a large number of your friends gathered at St. Matthew's Church in Oakville to say our final farewell to you. And now we struggle to deal with our loss. You may be gone in one sense, Milan, but your place in the hearts and minds of those of us who were blessed to know you is secure for all time. Your place in my heart will forever be yours. You have left your mark on me, and touched me more deeply than I realized while you were still here.

It is both painful and difficult to believe that we will not see you again in this lifetime. In some ways you were larger than life, Milan, and that is why your leaving has left us with such an empty feeling, and yet such a sense of gratitude at the same time. We were the fortunate ones whose lives were graced with your presence. You knew us and we knew you. You loved us and we loved you.

There are only a few people, Milan, who leave us with a memory that is so precious we know it will be with us for the rest of our days. You have given me the gift of such a memory. I will forever see you sitting there in our sailboat, a mere two and a half weeks before your death, with that beautiful smile on your face. You were more spirit than body that day, and that was so clear in your eyes. They seemed to be looking at us from some distant land. And the profound peace and the deep joy of another world were not waiting to show themselves. You were with us, more fully present than ever, but you were also seeing more than we could see, and loving us with such a pure love. In some ways your heart had already gone on ahead.

Your grateful friend,
Phil

*August 21, 2014*

# Another Kind of Birth

*D*ear Ginny,

In a few weeks it will be thirty years since you walked into our lives. I still remember the first time I saw you. You gave me such a warm, friendly smile. Perhaps it was at that moment that we became friends. And we have never ceased being friends. We have only grown closer through the years.

We still have that lovely photo of you chatting with Uncle Leo's friend Lorne on the shores of Lake Ontario. And then there is that very special picture of you timing one of Margaret's contractions the day Jim was born. Robert and Susan were there beside you in our bedroom, where Margaret was realizing her wish for a home birth. And now you are moving towards a different kind of birth, your birth into eternal life. I am finding it difficult to grasp the enormous reality of this event that grows closer with each passing day. It is a moment that will change our lives forever. Your death will leave such an empty space in my life.

Margaret had tears in her eyes at one point during supper last night as she thought of you— thought of what you are going through these days. Of what is happening in your failing body, yes, but even more of the pain you must feel in your gentle, loving heart as you say your goodbyes. That must tear at your very soul. Like you, however, we are not without hope. We share your deep faith that death, like birth, is not an end but a beginning. Just as the unborn child would not choose the trauma of leaving the comfort of the womb, so do we shrink from the dark passageway of death. We know by faith, though, that death is but another birth canal. Once again we will emerge into light, this time into a light that will never be extinguished, for we will be with the Source of all light and love and joy. We will be with the One who first called us into existence. And we will be there to stay. Forever! And one day those we leave behind will join us, for that is their destiny as well.

And so, my friend, I want you to know that it is okay to take leave of us. Sure, we will cry. But our crying will come to an end. Slowly it will dawn on us that in a very real and meaningful way you are still with us. That, as one anonymous writer has said, "(those) we have loved and who have loved us, not only make us more human, but they become a part of us and we carry them around all the time, whether we see them or not." We will certainly carry you around with us, Ginny, for we have loved you and you have loved us. We will still be there in your heart, and you will be in ours. And we will all be at peace in the heart of God.

(Comparing death to birth is not original to me. I have heard two different speakers make this comparison.)

*April 27, 2009*

# Happy Birthday, Kathleen

$A$ single rose sits in a vase on our dining-room table. It is there in your honour on this, your sixty-second birthday, just days after you left us. Two short years ago Margaret and I were at your place for your sixtieth birthday celebration. Can it really be that you are gone? Or is it that you are here but in a way that we cannot see you as before?

As I walked back from the store a short while ago carrying a small bouquet of three red roses, I suddenly had an impulse to go up to a neighbour's door and give her two of the roses. She cares for her eighty-eight-year-old mother, who has Alzheimer's and lives with her. I told her that one of the roses was for her and the other for her mother. She immediately put them into separate vases. Then I told her about you and the fact that this was your first birthday in heaven, and asked her to look on these roses as a gift from you. After all, it was only because of you that I had picked them up. She seemed very moved by this thought. You see, Kathleen, you are still touching the lives of people here—in some cases total strangers.

I love to associate roses with those who have passed on. It was a man from your native England, G. K. Chesterton, who once wrote: "If tiny seeds in the black earth can grow into beautiful roses, what must the human heart become in its long journey to the stars?" We shall look today at that rose on our table and think of you and send you our love across this great divide that seems now to separate you from us. And this evening Margaret and I will raise a glass to you, and ask you to pray for us as we continue on our way towards the same home you have already found. Rest in peace, dear friend.

With all our love,
Phil and Margaret

*October 5, 2005*

*D*ear Tom,

Margaret and I were saddened to learn of your father's passing. We might have learned of this sooner had we not been away from our parish some weekends in October.

The death of a parent has such a profound effect on the whole of our being. We are affected on every level by the loss of this person who has been a part of us from the very beginning of our existence. All the days and months and years of our life have been marked by the constant presence of this figure who has always seemed in some ways larger than our own life. And then for you, Tom, there is the added weight that goes with this loss of a second parent. I still recall the strange feeling of being all alone in the world when my mother died. My father had died some years earlier, and now the two people who had brought me into the world were gone. I felt like an orphan. Margaret and our children were there to love me and comfort me; I really wasn't alone, but I still felt so lonely. Abandoned, almost. It seemed that there was such a big hole in my life. Then the uneasy feeling of my own mortality came creeping in on me. As long as I had at least one of my parents around, there was this kind of security that my turn was still a long way off.

Ever so gradually my sense of the wonder and sheer joy of being alive worked its way back into my daily consciousness, and life became good again. Yes, both my parents were gone, but not without leaving me the greatest gift we humans are privileged to hand on: life itself. My own existence was the inheritance they had left me. I was truly "bone of their bone and flesh of their flesh," made in the image of God but in theirs too. Though there might be times when I would not always think of them, the rest of my life would in some way be my daily thanks for all they had given me. They would forever be mine and I would be theirs. And one day we would meet again and be surprised and delighted to find that in some deep and mysterious way we had really never been completely apart. I had always carried them with me in whatever I did and wherever I went in this world.

Phil

*December 2, 2008*

# Falling Sand

*I* lay there watching it happen. Watching those tiny white grains of sand fall ever so gently through that narrow opening. The movement was so constant, so steady, so unchanging. There was no rush to reach the tight passage to the other side, yet neither was there any hesitation. When it was your turn to fall through onto the pile below, away you went. And it all happened without a sound. I watched with the fascination of a child.

How long had this been going on? I knew the answer. How much longer would it continue? That I did not know. There was certainly more sand in the bottom than remained in the top. Yet I could not tell how long it would take the rest to work its way through such a narrow space. It was clear, however, that there would be no pause till there was only one pile. The longer I lay there, the less sand there would be to drop down. So I got up to start my day.

Even now, as my fingers touch these keys, tiny grains are lining up to take their turn down that slide. Others are getting off below. Is there anything I can do to keep this game from coming to an end? Should I simply be happy that I got a chance to play? What do I do with this longing to go on playing forever? The child in me has never wanted any game to end. God, can I have just five more minutes? Please.

*January 28, 2009*

# Not Tomorrow

"It won't be tomorrow," she said. By now Ginny knew that the cancer would eventually have its way with her, that it would rob her of the years ahead she had always assumed would be hers. But she also knew that it wouldn't happen tomorrow. She still had today and almost certainly the day after as well. Living in the present was now the only option left to her, and she found such peace in living like that. She would be thankful for the now of each day and the comforting assurance that she would have tomorrow too. All of reality was to be found within this very limited horizon. This was where she could still love God and those whom God had given her to love. Anything beyond this was no longer her concern.

There were times when Ginny would voice her gratitude for the grace of seeing life in this unfamiliar way. Even if the cancer were suddenly to disappear, she would not want to lose the peace that came from receiving the precious gift of each new day with such a grateful heart. And leaving all the rest to God.

If only we could have this blessing without the cancer, or whatever else it is that threatens to shorten our time here on this glorious Earth. Why do we always have to be looking so far down the road? Or looking back to where we've been? Trading away the present for a future that seems so distant or a past that we cannot regain. Living neither here nor there. Never fully attentive to the moment that is flowing quietly through us as we look beyond it to another time and place. So restless for the new or nostalgic for the old that we squander the treasure we already hold in our grasp. Unable (or is it unwilling?) to be like the One who dwells in an eternal *now*. And whose only name is *I AM*.

*December 22, 2009*

# You and Paul

*M*y dear Carolann,

Your birthday yesterday. Paul's today. You older by one year and one day. Your mother's womb would have still held its memory of your presence when Paul arrived to claim that space as his. Both of you offspring of Tony and Dolly. Sister and brother.

I am sorry, Carolann, that you now have to carry the pain and sadness that Jason spoke of yesterday. It is not fair that you and Paul have been torn apart in this way. Death had no right to do this, to be so cruel. But it will not have its way forever. Mortal bodies can break down and disappear, but there is more to us than feeble flesh. There is more to us than can be seen. "What is essential is invisible to the eye," as the author of *The Little Prince* reminded us. "It is only with the heart that one can see rightly." Even an aching heart can see that we must be made for more than this. An aching heart sees it best of all.

What was essential between you and Paul has not died. A part of that reality may have, but not the deepest and most important part. He is still your brother. You are still his sister. The Paul who has gone from our sight did not become who he was without you. You did not become who you are without him. If those who knew him for only a time can say that they are somehow different because of him, that he left his mark on them, with how much more reason can you say that he changed you in some way forever. We do not become ourselves all by ourselves. Those we love and those who love us help to fashion us into the persons we become. You carry Paul within you in ways you may not even know. He carried you in ways he may not even have imagined.

Some time back Paul wrote that he believed in heaven. I do not think his belief was born of the fear of the unknown, an unknown that seemed to grow closer with each passing day. Paul did not act out of fear. I think he believed in heaven because he believed in love, and sensed that love is stronger than death. He believed in love because he knew how deeply he loved, and found it inconceivable that that love would simply disappear with the death of his body. It was too real for that, too separate from his heart of flesh that one day would cease to beat. That kind of love must reside somewhere else. It is both inside us and outside us. In some way we are in it.

I do not quote Scripture as often as perhaps I should, though I do have some favourite passages. Here is one: "Eye has not seen, nor ear heard, nor has it entered into the human heart what things God has in store for those who love him" (1 Corinthians 2:9). If this is true, and I believe it is, then we can always say, "The best is yet to come." Scripture asserts that the test of how much we love God is how much we love others. The tributes to Paul over these past several days, and again today on his birthday, are all the testimony one would need to determine that Paul loved both God and everyone he ever met. His stated goal was to make all those he came in contact with not leave without feeling better about themselves. That is love at its finest—helping others to love themselves.

Each time you walk along the beach on Anna Maria Island, Paul will walk there with you. In some way he will be walking with you each day for the rest of your journey.

Love you,
Phil

*March 3, 2015*

# The Months of Our Lives

(from a speech on Gerry's seventy-fifth birthday)

*A* few weeks ago I was writing a note to a friend who was going to be away for a month. I suddenly found myself wondering how many months we have in a lifetime. How many do you think there are in a reasonably long life? I stopped and calculated: one thousand. Put that way, it doesn't sound very long, does it? A thousand months gets you to 83.3 years. Now all of us here are definitely going to live to our mid-nineties at least, if not to a hundred, but it is a sobering thought to realize that we get only a little over a thousand months in our lives. Especially as a few of us turn seventy-five this year and it dawns on us that we have already used up nine hundred of those months! The realization sure makes each one of them so very, very precious. Heck, I'm almost reluctant to turn the page on the calendar now. Think I'll just let October sit there through the first few days of November. Stretch it out a little.

However, there is no need to feel sorry for ourselves as we move further into what some call the golden years. The philosopher Seneca said that the gradually declining years are among the sweetest in life. And Joan Chittister, the Benedictine nun and author who turned seventy not long ago, wrote: "A blessing of these years is to wake up one morning and find ourselves drunk with the very thought of being alive."[8] Now notice that she didn't say that a blessing of these years is to wake up drunk. But surely she is on to something in her statement, and so is Seneca. There is a real sweetness in being drunk on being alive, in knowing the immense joys of family and friends, and in feeling rise within us an ever-deepening sense of gratitude to God for the great gift of life. Abraham Heschel once wrote: "Just to be is a blessing. Just to live is holy." I think we can all say "Amen" to that.

*October 24, 2008*

---

8   Joan Chittister, *The Gift of Years* (Ottawa, Ontario: Novalis, 2008), p. 31.

$D$ear Ellen,

I remember the day your family arrived from the west in the summer of 1949. Five of you and five of us in our small house made for a very cozy arrangement. Somehow it all worked out till you found your own place, and we were just happy to have you all back east. You were the cousins we knew we had but never got to see. Now you were here.

You were all of fourteen back then, Ellen. It's not true that I left home a few months later to get away from you. It had already been arranged that I would go to the Christian Brothers training college near Toronto in September of that year. However, my sister Mary kept me well informed about all the twists and turns in your life after I left. And Margaret and I have been fortunate to see you often over these past several years. It's been quite a ride, hasn't it? When I look at all the places you and Tony and your growing family lived and all the things that you have accomplished, I am more than impressed. I am somewhat in awe and proud to say that you were my cousin. Glad that we both shared the same degree of that good Devlin blood.

I could simply list all of your accomplishments, Ellen, but I'd prefer to focus on the person behind the accomplishments. And on the way you did not let the difficulties you had to face overwhelm you. Instead of running away from the hardships that came your way, you turned toward them and ran with them. You plunged right in and became part of the solution rather than part of the problem. If you knew of a young woman who needed a family during her teenage years, you would make her part of your family. If a young man needed a place to call home, your home would be that place. If schizophrenia was going to touch your family, you would face it head on and become president of the schizophrenia society. If there were people in your environment who needed personal care in their declining years, you would become a personal care worker. Someone has said that in the heart that is filled with love there is always room for one more. You found your joy in giving, and that is why you approached life with a wide open heart. And with that lovely smile on your face. In the midst of hardship and suffering you always saw the person, not the problem, and knew that your happiness was bound up with theirs.

How did you do all this when your heart must have been heavy with its own concerns? I think I know. The American sociologist Peter Berger wrote a book entitled *A Rumor of Angels*. In that delightful book he speaks of things in this life that point toward a life beyond this one. Among other things, he speaks of laughter as one of those signs of transcendence that marks humans as creatures who by their very nature are spiritual and are in themselves rumours that there is more than we can see here. Ellen, you had one of the best laughs that I have ever heard. That is why I loved telling you jokes, some even just a touch on the naughty side. I will miss that laugh. Your laugh was so full, so spontaneous, so almost musical. Whoever first spoke of "the lilt of Irish laughter" must have had someone like you in mind. There was such an uncontrolled, childlike, innocent quality in your laugh that I am sure Peter Berger would have agreed it was a rumour of angels. It somehow pointed beyond the here and the now. If you could laugh like that in the face of all the heartache life threw your way, life must have a deeper meaning than what we see on the surface. You did what you did, Ellen, you were who you were, because of a strong faith in God that carried you through all of life's ups and downs. Léon Bloy, who lived in France around the year 1900, once wrote: "Joy is the infallible sign of God's presence in a person." No wonder you were able to smile and even laugh in the midst of life's challenges. You were not alone and you knew it.

I was privileged to speak at your 75th birthday party, just seven short years ago. I reminded you then that our way of speaking about age is all upside down. We don't grow old. We grow young. We call babies and little children young because they are still so close to their beginning. To their Source. They are fresh from the hand of God. Why shouldn't we speak of those close to going back to God as young for the same reason? They too are close to their Source, to the God who first called them into being.

Each time Margaret and I visited you here in Barry's Bay during the past couple of years, Ellen, we always found you still able to smile through your aches and your pains, still animated as you spoke of some happy event, still able to laugh at my jokes. You even told John just a few days ago that I was one of the best joke tellers in the family. I was pleased to see that your mind was still sharp and that you hadn't lost your good judgement. I'll carry that compliment to my own grave.

I said to someone just the other day that God doesn't make photocopies. You are the only you there is, Ellen, the only you God made. We shall all miss you. Know that you have left your mark on each of us, and that we look forward to the day when we will see your smiling face again and hear that laugh one more time. God speed, Ellen, God speed.

With my love and admiration,
Phil

*March 7, 2017*

# Alyssa's Farewell

*A* mother lifts her young child up to the coffin. The soft, tender lips of a two-year-old kiss the cold, lifeless cheeks of her grandmother. Tiny arms reach out to give one last hug. Death does not hold her back from loving the one who used to hug and kiss her. She knows things are not the same now. She knows, too, that this is still in some way her Nama. The eyes may be forever closed, the mouth may no longer speak, but no one has to tell her who this is. What her young heart senses, and an older mind will one day come to understand, is that this body was the home of a beautiful soul. Out of here came love, endless amounts of it. A love that made her aware that she was special. A love that had been building up for years for the first one who would call her Nama.

Now it was time to say goodbye. Would she remember this moment? Perhaps not in a conscious way. But her young soul knows it has been deeply loved, and that kind of love has a way of leaving a mark that lasts a lifetime.

*October 12, 2005*

*I* walked into the kitchen this morning, a bit after seven o'clock, and kissed Margaret. That's our usual routine in the early part of our day, a little custom I started a few years ago. No point waiting till one of us is about to walk out the door to share a kiss when there are lots of days now when neither of us is leaving very soon.

It must have been my keen awareness that this was Ash Wednesday that prompted me to say just after we kissed, "Isn't it something to realize that someday these lips of ours will be cremated." Was I being morbid? Not at all. Just being real. Two hours later we would be together at Mass and we would have ashes placed on our foreheads in the sign of the cross with these sobering words: "Remember that you are dust and to dust you will return." The lips too. Is the Church being morbid? Not at all. Just being real. Only those who are free enough to look their mortality in the face are free enough to embrace the fullness of life that Jesus came to bring us.

Shortly after my unusual remark, Margaret said to me, "You are small town Ontario meeting up with grace." I am still not completely sure what she meant (you will have to ask her), but it seemed to be something positive. I like these words of James in 4:14: "For you are a mist that appears for a little while and then vanishes." Makes me want to squeeze every ounce of living out of every minute of every day. With a prayer of praise and thanksgiving on these lips.

*March 5, 2014*

# One Last Kiss

*I*t was a cold November morning in Ottawa. Six of us had just placed Anna's coffin over her open grave. It sat there waiting to be lowered into the ground. People pulled their collars up for further protection against the biting wind. The priest began the usual prayers at the cemetery, and we joined him in reciting the Lord's Prayer. Despite the cold, a part of me did not want this time to pass. I did not want to say a final goodbye to this cousin I had come to love so dearly.

Anna's son and daughter stood there, hearts heavier than anyone's. They had lost their father years earlier. Now they would be alone in a way they had never been before. Even adults can know what it is like to be an orphan.

The prayers were over and we all remained there in silence, lost in our own thoughts. Suddenly the daughter knelt down and kissed her mother's casket. Is it the mind or the heart that takes its own picture of such a fleeting moment and files it forever? I still carry that image so vividly. Lips touching varnished wood for merely a second, yet saying so much. How many kisses had this woman given to the one whose body lay suspended over that open grave? Kisses that stretched so far back in time. Way too numerous to count. This one would have to travel to the farthest reaches of the universe in search of a soul now on its way to the stars. The body in which son and daughter had taken their first tiny steps onto the human scene was now devoid of spirit. Anna was no longer there.

They say that love alone survives death. The love of those left behind surely does. And sometimes a kiss still says it all.

*December 19, 2010 (one month since the day Anna left us)*

# Reminders

*I*t happened in the Chimo Hotel in Ottawa. I was standing there combing my hair after a shower when I spotted the lines—little etchings that run out from the corner of my eye. Some head down my cheek, others go back towards my ear. Why hadn't I noticed them before? Perhaps the edge of my glasses had been hiding them. Why were they so visible now? Was it because of the way the light from outside struck that mirror?

A slight shock went through me. My face was older than I thought. Those "smile lines" were no longer there only when I smiled. They are just there. They are now a permanent part of me. They have taken up residence.

Should I mind? Not really. We can be friends, they and I. From now on they will tell me daily that I have already covered a lot of the road. They will say too that I have laughed often and smiled at many along the way. That is good. And, yes, they will carry the message that the road ahead grows ever shorter. And that is good too. Daily reminders of just how precious each day will be. There are so many more laughs to share and so many more faces to smile on.

*January 11, 2000*

# Part 6

*Christmas and New Year's*

# The Word

"In the beginning was the Word, and the Word was with God, and the Word was God." For years this opening verse of the Gospel of John made no sense to me. Each time I heard it read I was puzzled by it. Why did John refer to Jesus as "the Word"? How can a person be called a word? Was it because Jesus spoke words about God as no one else ever had? Somehow there seemed to be more to it than that.

The first bit of insight came one day as I was reflecting on the experience of writing. There were times when I sensed that the words I wrote seemed to come from somewhere below the reaches of my conscious mind. Did they exist in some form even before they reached the stage we call "words"? We are all familiar with the struggle that takes place within us during times of intense emotion as we search for the means to give expression to what is coming from the depths of our being. There are moments when we can almost feel something working its way up from far below the surface and demanding that we give it a name, that we clothe it in speech, that we let it become word.

It took a poet, Robert Frost, to finally put it together for me when he said that a poem begins with a lump in the throat. Now it all made sense. Jesus is the lump in God's throat as God looks out on poor, sinful, suffering humanity. Jesus is God's poem, a poem of love from deep within the Trinity, addressed to all of humankind at the same time as it is addressed to each one of us personally. God speaks Jesus. He truly is the Word. John did have it right.

Loyola House
Guelph, Ontario

*December 6, 2004*

*T*hey began as two separate reflections, one regarding peace and the other regarding adoration.

First I thought of peace, since that was the greeting bestowed on the shepherds the night that Christ was born. But just what is peace? It must be more than a negative concept, more than the mere absence of discord or hostility. Saint Augustine defined peace as "the tranquility of order." That is such a rich definition. How does it apply to the human person?

It seems to me that there is order in a person when all of his or her life's forces are flowing in one—and only one—direction. When her being is grounded in an Absolute, but in an Absolute that is personal, that one can relate to in love. When all the elements in a person are thus focused, when all her loves are but one Love, then there will be order in her being, and she will know the tranquility of order that is called peace.

I was still pondering this question of peace as we entered church and began to sing "Adeste Fideles." The refrain, *"Venite adoremus,"* led me to a deeper level: "Come, let us adore." We so seldom think of that word. I adore ... I recognize in You the answer to the deepest longings of my being. I recognize in You the final goal of my existence and the ultimate resting place of every human heart. I recognize that You alone are God. I adore. I am Yours and I am at peace.

The person who is grounded in this way will be free to love. Having come to know and befriend himself in the depths of his own being, he will be able to stand side by side with another as they look beyond themselves in a shared vision. Because he has found himself, he will be free to give himself. And giving oneself is love. Could this be what Gabriel Marcel meant when he said that love is the meeting of two freedoms?

*December 25, 1968*

$D$ear Amber and Adrian,

This is such a special Christmas for the two of you. You are now engaged, betrothed as they used to say in times long past. I like old words. They remind us of old values, values that are sometimes lost sight of in today's society.

Will there be presents carefully wrapped and placed under a tree? Perhaps dropped off at each other's home. On this first of so many Christmases will there will be a gift waiting to be unwrapped so it can add its voice to the message "I love you and I am so eager to spend my whole life with you. I am your betrothed, promised in marriage to you. Pledged to be yours in the most total and intimate and forever kind of way that one human being can belong to another"? Is that perhaps the real present under the tree this year? The one that needs no fancy paper to make it look special because there is no paper fancy enough for that. "I am yours. I am God's gift to you this Christmas. And you are God's gift to me. The One who stepped out of eternity and into time to show us how to love has led us to each other. We are called to be a sign of that great everlasting Love."

Margaret and I, all of us who know you, rejoice with you this Christmas. This first of so very, very many.

Phil

*December 24, 2016*

Margaret and I and Bart's parents had gathered at Bart and Michelle's early Christmas morning to be there when Emma and Leo, and to a lesser extent Owen, opened their presents. Emma and Leo could hardly wait to get started. They had left out cookies and milk for Santa the night before and even some carrots for the reindeer. Sure enough, those goodies were gone in the morning when they checked, so they knew he had definitely come and left presents for them. The moment they had been waiting weeks for was now here. They would finally see what Santa had brought them. It was decided that six-year-old Emma would pass out the gifts. Leo doesn't read yet.

She ran to the tree and didn't even seem to look at the name on the gift she grabbed. I immediately thought she must have already been peeking to see which presents were for her. I was wrong. Delightfully wrong! A few weeks earlier she and Leo had been at a craft store where they helped to make a stuffed dog for Owen, and they had recorded on the mechanical heart they put into the dog "We love you, Owen." Her young, generous heart of flesh couldn't wait to give their gift to her baby brother and have him hear those words. I knew right then that a child was showing us what Christmas is all about: the birth of Love and the way we can sometimes forget ourselves and be like the God who forgot about being God.

*December 26, 2007*

# A Hidden Present

$D$ear Cheryl,

Margaret and I were at first shocked when we received Amanda's e-mail yesterday telling us of your recent cancer diagnosis. I say "at first" shocked because I agree with Amanda's comment that there are "lots of reasons to be optimistic." You can still live out a normal life span with this thing, Cheryl. I spent last evening Googling "non-Hodgkin lymphoma" and called my friend Paul in Ottawa this morning. Ten years ago he was diagnosed with mantle cell non-Hodgkin lymphoma, a slightly different strain than yours, but he was already at stage four when they found his. The doctor put him on a strong chemo treatment, and here he is ten years later and feeling fine. He's not even on any medication. He was by himself at their cottage this morning when I called him. Yes, there are lots of reasons to be optimistic. I'm glad they caught yours early and that your treatment will be a milder form with fewer side effects.

The word *cancer* is such a terrifying word. We fear the worst when we hear it. However, there are hundreds of thousands of people who survive cancer and go on to live just as long as they would have lived without cancer. Keeping everything in perspective always helps. I love to quote the anonymous wise person who jokingly said, "We shouldn't take life too seriously; we'll never get out of it alive." I often think that the mystery isn't that we don't get to stay here forever; the mystery is that we ever get to be here at all. For me life is the great mystery, not death. A part of me never ceases to be somewhat in awe over the fact that I came to be. That, like you, I was given the immense joy of knowing and being known, of loving and being loved. That I have been moved beyond words by the beauty of a sunset or the innocence in a child's face. That my heart has been warmed by the smile of a total stranger. That my ears have thrilled to the glorious harmony of the human voice or the cheerful song of a robin on a spring morning. Despite all the ugliness and hatred in our world, one moment of simple human kindness, or an experience of unsurpassed beauty, touches me at a deeper level than all the evil out there. "Every experience of beauty points to infinity," as von Balthasar reminds us. We dwell in mystery.

I suspect, Cheryl, that you will know an even greater joy this Christmas than in other years. It will be because of a renewed appreciation of the incredible gift of life. You will have a keener sense of the sheer joy of being alive, of being able to love and be loved. That will be the present hidden under what seemed at first like a setback, an obstacle to your happiness. The joy you already derive from loving in the wholehearted way you do will seem to come from an even deeper Source. And in some way it will, because you will be more aware than ever before that Life itself is Christmas. That the gift of *you* was there under the tree the day you were born. God's first gift to you was *you*. A gift to all of us as well.

With my love and admiration,
Phil

*December 9, 2015*

# Of Pepper Shakers and Other Things

$W$oke up early on this first morning after Christmas. Not quite sure why. Perhaps because the little boy inside is still full of the joy of yesterday. No new toys to play with—just a heart that is eager to keep on celebrating.

Decided to start off with a cup of Ovaltine, a drink my mother used to love. Picked up one of those two identical mugs that always remind me of Amanda. They are favourites of mine as well. Noticed the Caffrey's beer glass that brings me back to the St. Patrick's Day when Fabe and I shared a pint together in our old neighbourhood. You got to keep the glass that day. I open mail with that lovely souvenir that Laurie brought back from South Korea. Hard not to think of her as I slit open each envelope. And then there is the pepper shaker. How often it makes me think of my mother and her fondness for pepper. And how much she minded the doctor's suggestion that maybe she should cut back on spices—yes, including pepper. "How can you eat a soft-boiled egg without putting pepper on it?" she would ask.

How many people in our world will come across some little object today and have it bring to mind a loved one, still here or now gone? How many will know a moment when the simplest thing will touch the heart with love in the gentlest of ways? Strange, isn't it, but marvelous too, how things can become more than things.

*December 26, 2008*

*D*ear Susan,

I enjoyed our brief conversation on Monday, the day you actually turned fifty. You know how much I would like to be there with Margaret and the others tomorrow when they officially celebrate your arrival at this half-century mark. However, I will be in Pembroke helping to welcome my sister into the ranks of the senior citizens.

I still recall with gratitude your and Robert's presence at my fiftieth birthday celebration way back in May 1983. (You were all of thirty-two back then.) The intervening years have given me a lot of time to reflect on this whole question of aging, of growing old. And you know, Susan, I think we have it all upside down. Let me explain why I say this.

We measure how young we are by how close we are to our birth. And we measure how old we are by how far we are from that moment. But that's only part of the picture—the surface part. To be born is to be freshly arrived from the Source of our being. To grow "old" and to die is simply to reverse the process. It is to grow back towards the Source of our being. To once again be close to our Beginning. And isn't that what it means to be young?

I have no difficulty in saying, Susan, that you are growing young. There may be days when your joints and your muscles tell you otherwise, but don't believe them. They don't know the whole story. Listen, instead, to your laugh. That's one of the things I listen to. It's one of our signs of transcendence, one of those "rumours of angels" Peter Berger used to write about. Your laugh is young. In fact, I think it's even younger now than back in those early days after Margaret and I first met you and Robert and I took delight in telling you jokes just to hear you laugh. And your heart is young, and getting younger. Lots of loving, genuinely caring for others the way you do, tends to have that effect on a heart. And your attitude towards life is young— refreshingly young. No sign of any hardening of arteries there.

All of this simply confirms that with each passing year you are growing closer to your Beginning, to the One who is eternally young. I was thinking these past few weeks that Christmas is not simply about Jesus' birth. It's about our birth too. Our call to be born again and again and again. Until we get to be so young that we just have to go off and rejoin our Beginning. Who is also our End. But don't get excited; you're nowhere near young enough for that yet.

So, Susan, if anyone so much as hints that at fifty you are at least getting close to being old, you just sit them down and tell them the real story. And from miles away I will raise a glass tomorrow to my young friend Susan, and to the sound of her laughter.

I love you, my friend.
Phil

*January 12, 2001*

# A Christmas I Can Never Forget

*I* was in grade four that Christmas Eve of 1942. And I still believed in Santa.

My brother and I had now been altar boys for over a year, and we would be in the sanctuary with the others for Midnight Mass. This merely added to the excitement of it all. Perhaps Santa would come while we were away at church. There might be presents when we got back home. I can still hear the nun who was in charge of the altar servers saying to my mother after Mass, "They must be so eager to see if Santa has already come." Years later my mother would tell us how painful it was for her to hear those words. She knew that Santa had not come, and that he was not going to come. My father was out of work and there was no money for presents. My brother and sister and I would have to learn the truth that our parents had struggled to hide from us.

We were not surprised to see that there were no presents yet when we got home. There was still time for Santa to come. And the fact that there was no Christmas tree did not upset us. We never had one in those years. So off to bed we went, quite confident that when we got up there would be something special for each of us. It was now almost the middle of the night, and we had no trouble falling fast asleep.

I do not remember my immediate thoughts or feelings on coming down in the morning to find that Santa had not arrived. I must have realized that, for whatever reason, he wouldn't be coming. It was now too late. Santa did not come in full daylight. This would be a Christmas without any presents. It is what followed that amazes me even to this day.

There were two rocking chairs in our family, one larger than the other. Two rocking chairs and three children was not a happy combination. So many of our fights were over those chairs. I do not know why things were different that Christmas morning. For some reason my brother and I squeezed into the larger chair and left the smaller one for our sister. That image of the three of us rocking happily away together remains so vivid in my memory. However, it is not only the fact that we were doing this so peacefully that still surprises me. It is the joy that I recall feeling at that moment. Where did we get this awareness that simply because it was Christmas we should be happy? That there was something so marvelous about this day, so very special, that even if you received no presents at all you still had lots of reason to be happy? It is now sixty-seven years later, and I have no explanation for the joy I felt that day. I don't think I ever will. And that is part of the beauty of it all. Beauty often seems to have some mystery attached to it.

As we ate the small roast of beef the butcher had given to my father on credit, I turned to him at one point and said, "There really isn't any Santa, is there?" He didn't reply. His smile said all I needed to know.

*December 7, 2009*

# Another Christmas

*H*ere it is, Christmas Day once again. By midnight tonight another Christmas will have become part of the history of our lives—these lives that move along at their own relentless pace. We can neither slow them down nor make them go faster. The speed of this current that carries us along never varies. Sometimes I stare at the second hand on my watch. I've tried telling it to stop, to take a pause. I don't want the precious days of my life to be passing so swiftly. It just ignores me.

In some philosophy class many years ago, I learned that time is nothing in itself. It has no existence of its own. Time is simply the measurement of change. No change, no time. All I need do is look at a few photos of myself over the years to be confronted with the undeniable reality of change. Time—and the camera—do not allow me the illusion of believing that it is only my surroundings that are no longer quite the same as they once were. The *I* of this entity I call my *self* keeps demanding to be reintroduced. Self, meet your new self. You are not who you were yesterday, you know. And certainly not the one who called himself *I* a year ago this day.

Why does Christmas put me in such a pensive mood? Me and those of us who have accumulated a significant number of Christmases past. No other season of the year so consistently brings to mind all those we love. Those we carry in our hearts each and every day, even on the days they don't happen to come to mind. Some of them were still here last Christmas; now they have gone home to God. The beautiful landscape of my earthly journey keeps changing. Some depart, others arrive. This year has been no different.

In June we said goodbye to our dear friend Mary Anne. She leaves such a void in the lives of so many of us. Mary Anne joined my life when she came to teach at Senator O'Connor back in 1974. We have been friends ever since, moving in and out of each other's life at regular intervals, always expecting a fresh joke at each new encounter. She is the one who gave Margaret a teaching position at Mary Ward, a unique school that owes its existence to Mary Anne's vision and determination. A truly remarkable woman, loved and admired by so many. We both miss her. Always will.

My good friend Milan took leave of us this past summer, though not before giving us the unforgettable privilege of taking him sailing on Lake Ontario a mere two and a half weeks before his death. That day will remain with me forever. Never have I seen anyone so serene and joyful mere days before leaving this earth. Still in love with the now, yet filled with confident anticipation of the not yet. The shore he could already see was not the one on that day's horizon.

But this life goes on, and others arrive to keep us aware that our time here is good too. Immeasurably good. Mary Anne knew the immense joy of having her brand new nephew lie right there against her heart just days before that heart beat for the last time. The baton of life was being handed on to one of the new runners in the race.

Our own son welcomed our newest grandchild into the world just two short months ago. We give thanks for the gift of her life, with full awareness that only a part of our lives will overlap with hers. That is the way it is meant to be. Life gives birth to life and the incredible miracle goes on and on. And on.

So this is Christmas Day. Those two words have such a special ring to them. They are magical. But why? A few weeks ago a Facebook friend posted this statement by C. S. Lewis: "I believe in Christianity as I believe that the sun has risen; not only because I see it, but because by it I see everything else." As I reposted the quotation, I added that some wise man once said, "Some things have to be believed to be seen." I was sure that C. S. Lewis had experienced the truth of those words. What keeps the magic of Christmas alive even when we have lost touch with the day's origin and its ultimate meaning? It's because we still know that this day is all about Love. Our giving comes out of our deep desire to say, "I love you." And thus we bake and we sew and we send cards, and we shop for the perfect gift, all because we want to see the smile on the other's face, or know that we have warmed another's heart. We want to experience the joy of giving. Of loving. We have a profound sense that when life is stripped bare of all that does not matter, it really is all about loving and being loved. And Christmas says this in a way that no other day does. What our mind may have lost sight of, our heart still remembers: Once upon a time, Love was born and came to dwell among us. And I have been made in that image. I have been made to love. That is why I am happiest when I am loving. Yes, even more than when I am being loved, however wonderful I know that to be. I carry the meaning of this day at a depth that nothing can reach, nothing can erase.

And so I will savour each of the sweet and gentle moments of this day, another of the many Christmases of my life. I will rejoice with those who are with me today, and I will think of all those I love who are not with me. I will give thanks for the joy of giving and the joy of receiving. And I will let my mind and heart go back to the first Christmas of all, to the one that had to be before any of us would be celebrating this one.

Christmas blessings and love to all of you,
Phil

*Texas*
*December 25, 2014*

# My Wish for You, My Friend

*T*his is the first day of a brand new year of your life and mine. My heart is telling me that it wants to send you a special greeting, but my mind does not yet have the words. What should I say to you today? This day that seems so much like all the others, yet seems in some way so very different. Should I say that I am glad you are my friend? Yes, I want to say that. But I want to say a great deal more. Whether you joined my life long ago or during this year that has just come to a close, I want to wish you something special on this day of new beginning.

So what do I wish for you? I wish that each day, each week, and each month of this year be a time of growth for you. Whether you are still young in years, at the midpoint of your journey, or into the autumn of your life, I hope that you keep right on growing into you. None of us has arrived; no one of us is there. Nor will we ever be this side of eternity. Go forth to meet yourself each day, confident that on that same road you will meet Another who dwells in the deepest and most authentic part of you. Grow in the direction of that inner Presence. Do not settle to be who you were yesterday. It is always today, and each dawn calls for a new you. You have to be born again and again and again. Do not shrink from the pain of your own birthing. If the journey seems too difficult at times, if each step feels like your last, look back to see if the footprints behind are really yours.

Let yourself be led gently along the path of your own becoming. Anxious striving does not help. The growth of the inner you continues on in silence without our even being aware of it. Ever so slowly, imperceptibly, we grow in the direction of our longing. We need only be vigilant about the things we love, for that is where we are destined to arrive. The contents of our hearts will always be more important than anything we possess.

And so, my friend, what I wish for you today is you. The you of your ceaseless longing to be more.

*January 1, 2010*

# Part 7

*Friendship*

# The Point of You

"What is the point of me?" you ask. I feel dumb before the question. I know it is in some ways the only question there is, the only one worth asking. Beside this one, all the others seem so trivial.

I know there is a point to you, but I feel so lost when I try to find the words to bring that to the surface. Some answers seem to lie even deeper than the questions. What is the point of you? Well, what would be missing if you were not here? Let's start by asking that. Let me put the question to those who love you. What would they say? Where would that love go if you were not here? Only you can call forth that particular love from their hearts. It is not there for anyone else, however many others they may love. And what about those you love? Could anyone else give them your love? Silly question, isn't it? Only you can give the world the love that is yours alone to give. Because you are the only you there is—in the whole universe! The ones you love now, the others who will come along to make a claim on your heart, they all depend on you. It is your love they long for; it is in your heart they hope to find a home.

It may be that you will one day bring new, young lives into our world. If that comes to pass, they will have no doubt about the point of your existence.

And yet this is not something you have to do to prove your worth. Your value is rooted more deeply than even that. It goes back to the time when you were being "knit together in your mother's womb" (Psalm 139:13). We arrive with the point of our existence already built in. We are here to give our love to others and to receive theirs in return. But that seems all too wonderful to be true, and far too simple. Do I really have something of value to give to others? Me? And am I really lovable? Is there any point to me? Does it matter that I am here? Sometimes I wonder if at some unconscious level we are all asking each person we meet "Do you love me?" There is a part of me that will always be astonished that others do love me. It's as though I can't quite believe it, regardless of how often I see that they do. It just seems too much to believe, because it is so special.

Nevertheless, I have come to believe it. Yes, I am lovable; it matters that I am here. And it matters that you are here. The point of you is you. It is the joy that you bring to the world just by being. And it doesn't depend on anything you do. The value of what you do flows from who you are. Fall in love with you.

I love the you that you are.

*July 8, 2008*

# Eulogy for David Thompson

*S*hortly after 8 a.m. on Thanksgiving Day, Jane called from Florida to tell me that her father had died earlier that morning. Though her call was in some ways not a surprise, it still came as a shock to learn that this wonderful man had taken leave of us. It was sad to think that I would never again hear his voice, nor would my wife and I have the pleasure of dropping in for a visit on our next trip to Ottawa. I hung up the phone with a deep sense of personal loss, and sadness that Jane and her brothers were now without their father.

It immediately occurred to me that in some way it was appropriate that David's heart would give out on the day we call Thanksgiving. There was a lot of gratitude in that heart, despite the sadness of not having his dear Margaret there beside him these past few years. He could still visit her, and know that in some unspoken way she derived comfort from his daily visits. He still had her to live for, and his children, and their children. As well as his friends, and good music, and the intellectually stimulating articles in *The New Yorker*. It struck me that morning how very much his family, and indeed all of us, have reason to give thanks for the life of this very special man.

I doubt that any of you would disagree with my brief text message to Jane later that day. I said simply that whoever first combined the words "gentle" and "man" must have had David Thompson in mind. I cannot think of anyone more deserving of that title. There was even a quality in his voice that seemed to come from some wellspring of gentleness at the very core of his being. If David was anything, he was a gentle man.

This does not mean, however, that he was too reserved to express his opinion if he felt that the people in charge of our country, or our province, were not conducting business the way he felt they should be. A little edge could creep into that gentle voice on those occasions. His mind was too sharp, and he was too well read, to hold back from expressing his views on the major issues of the day.

In the early '90s we acquired a sailboat, one large enough to safely accommodate five or six adults. We were pleased when David and Margaret eagerly accepted our invitation to come down to Toronto to go sailing with us. Alice Murphy, a cousin who was close to Margaret, came along as well. It took us over two hours to sail from the Scarborough Bluffs to the Toronto Islands. One of my fondest memories from later that day is seeing David relaxing in the cockpit of our boat as we left the islands to head back home. As we pulled away from the dock, we were facing the Toronto skyline on the far side of the harbour. Straight ahead of us, standing there among all those tall buildings, was the Scotia Plaza, the bank tower that David had spent five years of his life helping to design. He and Margaret had moved to Toronto so that he could be part of the team overseeing its construction. It was pride in his own craftsmanship that I could see on David's face at that moment. A significant fixture in the skyline of Canada's largest city bore his imprint.

In closing, I am going to take the liberty of making a gender change in a passage from Proverbs. Most of you have heard of the valiant woman who is spoken of in the last chapter of this book of the Old Testament. With your permission, and hopefully that of the author of this sacred text, I would like to adapt this passage as follows: "A perfect husband (and father)—who can find him? He is far more precious than jewels. His wife's heart has confidence in him; from him she will derive no little profit. Good and not hurt he brings her all the days of his life."

David, you have brought untold good to your dear Margaret, to your children, to their children, and to all of us. We are better for having known and loved you, and having been loved by you. We will carry you in our hearts for as long as we shall live, and even beyond. For love does not pass away.

*October 21, 2013*

*D*earest Cousin Margaret,

It was just one short week ago today. A number of us were huddled together against the bitter cold as the priest led us in the prayers around your graveside. We were there to say our final goodbye to you. Hands, feet, and faces were cold, but hearts were warm with our love for you. Heavy over our loss, but warm with the fond memories of you each of us carried. And will always carry. You have left your mark on us.

We find it hard to accept that we will not see you again in this life, even though we know that it was good for you to take leave of us at this time. Your last years here were not easy ones. You lived in that shadowland where you were no longer sure just who you were, or who we were. Now you know. And you know the name of that lovely man who used to come to visit you every day, and why he wanted so much to be there with you. Did you have some vague, uneasy awareness that something special was missing from your life when he suddenly stopped coming? Now you know what happened. Did his absence make you want to go find him? The way you once wanted to go find your childhood home. If he could no longer come to see you, you would go to see him. You found a way. In that we take comfort.

David's cousin, Father Larry, spoke so warmly during your funeral Mass of the times he would go to your place and you would serve him those delicious meals you prepared. I imagined how pleased David must have been on those occasions to have his beautiful wife treating his cousin to her fine cooking. As Fr. Larry continued speaking, my mind wandered off for a moment to the meaning of your name. You must have known that Margaret means *pearl*. I got to thinking that men don't wear pearls the way women do, but they can marry one. Your David certainly did, and I'm sure he knew it. You were the best thing that ever happened to him. And he was no doubt the best thing that ever happened to you. I know four people who would concur with these statements.

Beside me as I write, Margaret, is a copy of the stunningly beautiful photo of you taken when you were eighteen or nineteen. I think you were working in C. D. Howe's office at the time. Cathleen found it among Anna's things when her mother died, and she gave it to David. He had never seen this picture of you before and was deeply moved. It made him proud all over again that he had won the hand of so beautiful a woman. Your children, too, just love that photo of their mother. Many women would have made sure that picture was always displayed in a prominent place in their home. The fact that it was only discovered all those years later speaks to another kind of beauty, one that no camera can record.

Till we meet again.
Love, Phil

*December 23, 2013*

# A Precious Memory

$W$hy can I still remember that moment? My end-of-the-day grade nine French class had just been dismissed. I stood outside the Lynch building, watching the students as they headed over to the main part of the school. My eyes followed one in particular. Aware that I took a special delight in having her in my class, I reflected on what a beautiful young woman she was on the very threshold of becoming. I could sense even then the loveliness of the person who was emerging. At times I wondered if she knew how much I appreciated the warmth in the smiles she gave me. I knew we liked each other.

As I stood there watching her disappear that afternoon, it never crossed my mind that we were already on the way to becoming friends for life. Friendships are often born in such quiet, unobtrusive ways. Like the flowers they are, they silently appear on the landscape of our lives, bringing joy to our days and making us aware just how lovely a world this can be.

January 20, 1994

# An Odd Thank-You

"*T*hank you for your friendship," he said. The words seemed odd to me. Wasn't he my uncle, my mother's brother? Here he was in his early nineties, holding my hand as we walked down the hallway of the seniors' residence where he now lived. Never before had he called me his friend, and the word startled me a little. To me he had always been simply Uncle Leo.

It was on his farm between Perth and Smiths Falls that we had spent some of the best summers of our young lives. My brother and I used to take turns getting up around five o'clock in the morning to ride with him in his old truck, bringing milk from his neighbours' farms to the cheese factory. As we drove slowly along the deserted country road, he would sometimes ask us to hold the steering wheel for a moment while he lit one of his roll-your-own cigarettes. We loved to jump in the hay in the barn and some days actually helped to bring some in from the fields. I still remember feeling so big, so much like a real farmer, when I learned how to shout "coboss" to bring the cows in at milking time. At night we would often fall asleep to the comforting sound of Uncle Leo playing the fiddle. Those days seemed so far off now, part of another lifetime, as he and I walked hand in hand down that hallway.

It was true that he and I had grown very close over the years—especially these later years when we would bring him down to Toronto each June to spend time with Lorne, this dear man he had known all his life. How they enjoyed reliving so many cherished memories from a time long gone. The times when they would spell each other on the fiddle at those barn dances that would go on all night. We loved listening to them bring those days back to life.

Here we were now, a man in his nineties and another in his fifties. We had shared a lot. Through it all we had become friends, he and I. And that was somehow more than uncle and nephew. One came with birth. This other was of our choosing. Ties of blood are surely precious. Friendship does not come that way and deserved its own special thank-you.

*January 26, 1997*

# Love, Hate, Fear

*D*ear Carolann and Jim,

This is the first chance I've had to respond to your request for a few thoughts on "love, hate, and fear." Just reread Paul's excellent reflection on these realities we all know so well. We know them because we live them, but the articles Paul refers to, and his own thoughts, force us to go deeper and ask ourselves what we believe about the relationship between love and hate and fear.

The poet E. E. Cummings wrote, "Unless you love someone, nothing else makes sense." Interesting that he didn't say, "Unless someone loves you..." Being loved is certainly an essential step on the way to being capable of loving, but I believe that our greatest happiness comes from the love we give to others. Paul has to be aware that so many people love and admire him, yet it is his love for them that comes through so strongly when he writes. In this case, his love for Jackson Kai and also his "blood brother Tim" who, despite his MS, will be coming to see him next week. Paul doesn't love in the abstract; his love is for each person who has become a precious part of his life. Next he mentions Donna, who was coming to visit him that day. Paul seems to take even more delight in his love for his friends than in their obvious love for him. It is no wonder that his world still makes sense even though he lives daily with the awareness that his time here could end at any moment.

The articles Paul has been reading, plus his own deep thinking about the insights of these authors, have led him to move away from viewing hate as the opposite of love. He now sees fear as the great enemy of our ability to love: "the fear to let go and risk for love—for happiness." It has long seemed to me that we all carry this existential fear of losing ourselves if we let go and love someone. We want to escape the isolation of our incomplete selves, we want the intimacy that loving another will bring us, but we aren't ready to accept the risk of losing so much. We are not sure these others will love us. And if they don't, then what will we do? This is all we have. So we spend the early years of our lives in a tentative, hesitant manner. We keep hidden from our own eyes the question inside us as we approach each person we meet: "Do you love me?" We carry this question until the day we decide that we are good enough, that we are worthy of being loved, and then choose to be ourselves without undue fear of rejection. We let go. We risk. And we discover how wonderful it is to love and to be loved. To feel complete. To be happy.

Paul must have reached this stage some years ago. He would not have all these friends otherwise. He must have known this in some way the day he and Tim decided to become "blood brothers." However, there is a new depth in his awareness of this, and a new understanding of just how true it is. Paul derived considerable satisfaction from having his own insights articulated and confirmed by these respected sources. Paul could have saved Harvard all the years of research it took to finally arrive at the conclusion that having love in one's life leads to happiness. Institutions have this need to verify through statistics what we already know.

As Paul says, his mind seems to be at its best when he is not feeling well. He switches into this "nothing matters" mode, and he sees so starkly what really does matter, and then states, "It all has to do with love." Paul attributes his shedding of any last vestiges of fear, this other side of love's coin, to "the experience of not yet dying." He lives with death as a daily companion. Death is both his enemy and his friend. At the same time as it threatens his very existence, it gives him a clarity of vision that he might not have been able to obtain any other way.

Paul concluded his soulful reflection with these words: "Love and happiness and loss of fear is a super way to celebrate this (Valentine's) day." It sure is! So many of us are grateful to him for enriching our celebration of the day, and deepening our sense of what the day is really all about. No chocolates or flowers are a match for this kind of gift.

The French author Léon Bloy once wrote: "There are places in the heart that do not yet exist; suffering has to enter in for them to come to be." Those of us privileged to know Paul see clearly that the suffering of these past several years has fashioned his heart into one of rare beauty.

All my love,
Phil

*February 16, 2015*

*D*ear Sylvia,

I know that this is not a letter I can send to you by mail. You are no longer here to receive letters that way. However, I still want to write to you, more for my sake than yours.

John phoned last Sunday to tell me that you had died the day before. I could hardly believe what he was saying. Not Sylvia, my former student and friend of all these years. Still young and vigorous, involved in so many things. It did not seem possible. I should have realized that something was wrong when I did not hear from you at Christmas. You were always so faithful in sending a card and a letter and pictures of the family. Now I know why no card came this year. You had been ill for some time. I am sorry, dear friend, that I was not in closer touch.

Margaret and I drove to St. Thomas yesterday to be at your funeral. It did not surprise me that the church was packed with people from all walks of life, there to say goodbye to their former mayor. John and Erin spoke so beautifully and so movingly of you, and Father Poulin added his own words of admiration. I found myself sitting there with such a full heart and often with tears in my eyes—tears of pride in you, my friend, and tears at my own loss. You leave a hole in my life.

I was humbled on a few occasions yesterday, Sylvia, when John and Marion and other family members spoke of the way I had touched your life. It seems to have been more than I ever realized. Alex said that you and I went well beyond teacher and former student. His comment and those of others moved me deeply—left me feeling surprised and humbled and ever so grateful. And more keenly conscious of my loss.

I still recall the time you came back to see me at O'Connor when you were at university. You even sat in on one of my classes. Afterward we went to the empty teachers' lunchroom and you shared about the things going on in your life at that time, some of them quite personal. I sensed then that we were going to be friends for a long time. Years later I would have the privilege of being at your fortieth birthday party, where I gave you this silly book of photos of very elderly women with their beautiful, wrinkled faces and eyes still full of the mischief of youth. Not sure what you thought of that, but I wish now you had stayed around to grow old and have wrinkles. You escaped all that.

As we drove back from St. Thomas yesterday, my mind kept going over the wonderful things people said about you, and I found myself in admiration of the special person you had become and all you had accomplished. And then I started to dwell on the mystery of love and friendship and the ways in which people touch one another's lives without even being aware of it. We have not had all that much communication over these past few years, Sylvia. Now I wish it had been more. But we have made a difference in each other's life. However much I may have influenced your life, it is also true that you have impacted mine—and probably more than you were aware, or than even I was aware. Until these past few days.

There was a strong, unspoken bond between us that I am only now beginning to fully appreciate, and it did not require a lot of upkeep. It had been formed long ago and it had no expiry date. Way back there at O'Connor some intangible reality drew us together, and we became friends for life. From then on we mattered to each other. Not simply as teacher and student but as human being to human being. I had a place in your heart and you had a place in mine. That never changed. It never will.

***

It is now the Thursday after Easter. Don't know why I didn't finish this letter to you last week. Well, perhaps I do. It is partly due to the fact that I ran out of time and energy on that Good Friday night. However, I suspect that it is also due to my reluctance to say a final "goodbye" to you. As long as I kept "talking" to you like this, there was the comforting feeling that somehow you were still here, and I did not want to let go of that. Now I must accept that I will no longer see you in this world. That is not something I want to accept. It is being forced on me. I have no choice.

They say that we become what we love. I believe that we also become the ones we love. Somehow the people we take into our hearts have a way of slowly and imperceptibly leaving their mark on us and, without our even knowing it, their goodness changes us in some way. We become more fully the person we are called to be. As we all said farewell to you last Thursday, Sylvia, I had this sense that your goodness, your loving nature, had crept into some corner of my heart and soul years ago and had remained there ever since. All through the long spaces in our communication, you were there. And now you will go right on being there till it is my turn to go home to God. And to you.

I love you, my dear friend.
Phil

*April 8, 2010*

$D$ear Sheila (a nun friend and former teaching colleague who went home to God two years ago),

Thank you for sending us that beautiful piece, "The Lord Made Woman." I believe every word of it, and I feel blessed to have so many fine women in my life. This year I have the privilege of living with three of them: Margaret, my beautiful life companion; our daughter Michelle; and little Emma, who will be two and a half on Valentine's Day. It is delightful to watch her young womanhood emerge day by day in front of our eyes. This morning she ran into the living room, immediately spotted the new lamp that we came home with last night after she had gone to bed (and that I didn't think she would even notice—after all, it's not a toy), and then came up to me and said, "Thanks for buying it." We'll miss her when they move out this coming summer, but we've had two years of wonderful bonding.

I have long been conscious of how strongly I feel drawn to good women and sometimes suspect that it is the feminine side of myself that is behind this strong attraction. Michelle said to me a few years ago, "The feminine in you is more developed than in most men." I took that as a compliment.

At times I also think about the fact that God is the ultimate Source of all those qualities we sometimes designate as masculine or feminine. All that is good and wonderful in us creatures has to come from the Creator. In those moments I find myself wondering if my attraction to women is in some way a reflection of a deep hunger that lies buried within me for what I might call "the feminine side of God." I think it was Augustine who said, "A friend is the other half of my soul." I am conscious of woman as being in a special way that other half of my soul. I love all my male friends and could not do without them, but I am always aware of that mysterious and marvelous "otherness" that my women friends bring to my life.

Years ago I came across a description of success for a man that I wish now I had saved. What I remember is that one of the signs of being a successful man was being loved by good women. If there is any truth to that, then in this later stage of my life I can truly say that my life has been a success. I count among my close friends so many fine women whose love means such a great deal to me. You, dear friend, are one of them. You are such a good woman. I am so glad we connected again after several years of having been out of touch. It brings me much happiness to know that we can in some way share the rest of the journey home. God is good.

Love,
Phil

*February 12, 2004*

$D$ear Bas,

It is only two short days since you left us. You went off to meet God at 11:10 on Saturday morning. Margaret and I arrived just twenty minutes later. Your body was still warm when I leaned over to kiss your forehead. Our last visit had been one week earlier. You had no trouble eating the ice cream bar I brought you that day, and it seemed to go down more smoothly than the Harvey's hot dog I had brought you the week before. How you loved those Harvey's hot dogs! With nothing on them but a little mustard, and dills on the side. You told me once that when you were a boy in Windsor, your mother would always have a jar on the table filled with some of the dills she had pickled, and sometimes beets as well. You seemed to love more and more to let your mind go back to those early days of your life in Windsor, those days before you lost your mother at the young age of thirteen. That was a wound that perhaps had never completely healed over, until Saturday. It is healed now, Bas, healed forever. Her arms must have been the first to welcome you.

You came into my life way back in September 1948 when you and Brother Norman came to teach in Pembroke. I was all of fifteen then. You were just twenty-six. You know, Bas, if the Brothers had not come to Pembroke at that time, I doubt that I would ever have finished high school. I am sure that so many others could say the same thing. I would certainly never have become a teacher. You changed our lives. Over the past few years people have said at times that it was good of me to come and see you so often, that I was such a great friend to you. Each time they said that, I could not help but think of what I owed you. How many people come along in our youth and change our lives forever? Put us on a path to a much better education than we would ever have received, and leave us with an abiding sense of the place of God in our lives? And you not only did all that, you then became a lifelong friend—one with whom I was privileged to share a year in community and a few summers taking courses together. And when I was no longer officially a Brother, you opened your heart and your life to Margaret as well. You and your friend, Sister Ellen Leonard, even organized a wonderful reception for us here before our wedding in California. No, Bas, you didn't owe me; I owed you. And I always will.

Not everyone knows what a toll your bouts of depression took on you. That "black dog," as Churchill called it, didn't leave you alone for long. In earlier times you hid it well, but there were periods in your life when it got the better of you, and sometimes kept you from being your best self. You will be the first to admit that you weren't always easy to get along with during these last few months. Since your death, Bas, I have almost expected you to come to me in a dream and ask me to tell some people that you are sorry for having given them such a difficult time. It's okay; you don't need to. They understood, especially as they saw how much pain you had to deal with. We all live with more than a little concern about how well we will handle these things when our turn comes. Not everyone knows, either, that on some of those days when you were tossing from side to side in your bed and swinging your arms from one railing to the other, you were crying out through your pain, "Jesus, Mary, and Joseph, save souls." Over and over you banged the sides of your bed, and over and over you begged God to save souls. You said it was your friend Saint Theresa, the Little Flower, who had inspired you to say that prayer.

Do you remember the day, Bas, when we were driving along Queen Street and you thought someone was calling your name? It was a beautiful day in early May 2004, and you and I were driving down to the Beaches. I had phoned that morning and had come to pick you up because you were feeling down. I remember the day because I wrote about it in my journal. As we drove along Queen Street, you rolled down the window at one point and said, "Sometimes I think I hear my name being called." I thought to myself, *Your name is being called, Bas, but not in the way you think.* This was only two months before the stroke that would put you in a wheelchair for the rest of your days, and it was already evident that your once vigorous and athletic body was undergoing serious changes. It seemed so fitting that you were beginning to hear your name called. The voice of the One who had first called you into being was slowly becoming audible, barely discernible at that point, but entering your life again and preparing you to hear your name called once more. You have been listening so attentively for that voice these past weeks and months, and growing more than a little impatient at times. Was it a holy impatience? I recall the day a while back when you said to me, "This is taking longer than I thought." Just recently when I arrived for a visit, you said, "I've been ready the past two nights." I knew what you meant but I said anyway, "Ready for what?" You replied, "Ready to go and meet God." And now your prayers have finally been answered. I am glad for you, Bas. Sorry for me and the rest of us, but glad for you.

It's time to say goodbye, old friend. We can't do a high five anymore, but I can, for one last time, say goodbye in the way you so often liked to say goodbye. Check. Check, Bas, check.

Your friend,
Phil

*October 1, 2007*

# This Flower

*I*t's a one-of-a-kind flower, and it could so easily not have come to be at all. Some of life's most precious realities have hung by the tiniest of threads in their first tenuous moments. You needed a ride to your friend's music recital in Waterloo, and we had room.

We all sat there in rapt silence as Diana both delighted and amazed us with her ability to bring such sweet and powerful notes out of this long piece of metal with its various openings. Her fingers danced from one portal to the other as she breathed life into this inert object she called her flute. We were in awe at the level of achievement to which God-given talent and hours upon hours of hard work had brought her. The reception that followed was filled with expressions of deep admiration and the warmest of congratulations.

It was time now for the ride back home. Which one of us suggested that perhaps we should stay in touch? In any case, the desire to keep up the contact seemed to be a mutual one, and so we exchanged e-mail addresses.

Here we are now, several years later and so many steps further along the path of a unique friendship—a friendship between a man in the latter part of his life and a young woman still fresh with the beauty of youth. An old man with a young heart and a young woman with an old soul. This flower has taken its place on the human landscape. It knows it is but one among so many, but it knows that it is no less special because of that. It is "this flower," and there is no other just like it anywhere on the face of the earth.

This flower they can rightly call "ours" knows exactly where it is meant to stand in the garden. It makes no demands on them. It does not require attention that might take either of them away from anyone else. It knows so well that "love is the meeting of two freedoms," and simply rejoices in whatever little signs of love and friendship life brings its way. Because it knows that it is loved all the time, and not only when those who planted it have the leisure to stop by and notice its beauty.

Like all the flowers that dot our landscape, this flower will one day pass from sight. The day will come when the two who gave it life are no longer here. That does not mean, however, that there will be no trace of them or their flower. "Love never dies," we are told, and it will always make a difference somewhere that they met and chose to share some part of life's journey. Just as violence and hate tear our world down, so do friendship and love build our world up. It will always matter that they gave life to their flower. Always.

*June 14, 2010*

# Part 8

*Family*

# The Euchre Party

$S$he was in her early thirties, he in his late forties. Though they did not yet know each other, his sister Annie was about to change that. She organized a euchre party at her brother's place and invited Bessie to come along.

How many of you can trace back to a similar moment in time when your existence hung there in the balance, dependent on one person's saying yes to something as ordinary as a euchre party? It was long years later that I learned how my mother and father first came to meet. It is impossible for me not to wander back in time to Aunt Annie's invitation to this woman who would become my mother. What if Bessie had not known how to play euchre? What if she had just not felt like going that evening? Even now as I write these words, I am so very grateful that she said yes to that simple invitation. And I picture her and my aunt walking along those dusty Pembroke streets that led from the General Hospital where they both worked to the very modest house on Peter Street where my father lived with his elderly mother.

I wish I knew how the card game went that evening. Whether the man who would become my father ever had as his partner the woman his sister wanted him to meet. A year or more later he would write this woman a letter in which he spoke both of his love for her and the risk she would be taking in marrying an older man. He wrote of how the young may die but the old must. What thoughts went through her mind as she read of his concern? Fortunately, she was now ready to say yes to something of much deeper significance and of greater consequence than a euchre party. She would become Jim's wife and the mother of his three children.

How could I not be eternally grateful to this woman whose yes to a card game turned out to be the yes that my whole existence depended on?

*November 3, 2010*
*(the 112th anniversary of Elizabeth Devlin's birth)*

# Enduring Memory

*I*t is one of my most enduring childhood memories. I want to write about it, but I do not know if I can find the words.

The house where I grew up was not very big. At the top of the stairs on the second floor was an open space where my brother and I had our bed. To the right of the stairs was our sister's tiny bedroom. Next to that was our parents' room. It happened some nights that my father would go into their room first, close the door, and get ready for bed. My mother would come along later and pass through our area on the way into their room. In that split second before she closed the door behind her, I would sometimes catch a glimpse of my father. This is the memory that has never left me. He would be on his knees at the side of the bed, hands joined together and head bowed. In those years he still wore "combinations," as they were called, the long one-piece underwear that went from the shoulders down to the ankles. I know that at least on one occasion the back flap was partly open. That didn't matter to him. He was saying his prayers and was oblivious to everything else.

That scene seared itself into my memory. I was still a little boy at the time, and he was this big, strong man. So big and so strong that all he had to do was speak to me in a stern voice and tears would come to my eyes. I loved him and I feared him. I held him in awe. That is why I was so struck by the sight of him on his knees in this way. Now he was the little boy.

I doubt that there are any words he could have said that would have stayed with me the way that image has. In what strange, mysterious manner do these briefest of moments imprint themselves in the depths of our being and remain there forever? All I know is that from then onward I had the clearest impression possible of who God is and who I am. God is the Creator and I am the creature. God is where I began and where I am destined to return. And I need at times to get on my knees and acknowledge this most basic of all realities: I am not the author of my own existence. I am on loan to myself. I belong to Another.

*May 4, 2010*

# How Can We Tell Her

*I*t was somewhere in the early 1940s. My mother's great aunt had written, asking if she could come to live with us during her final years. She had made this same request of closer relatives, but none had room for her. And back then one had few alternatives apart from family if one could no longer manage living alone.

Before long Aunt Tressa and her piano left Trenton and arrived in Pembroke. My parents' bedroom became hers, and they moved their bed into a corner of our small living room. It all worked somehow.

I do not recall how long Aunt Tressa lived with us. I do recall the morning she died—right there in her bed, in the room next to the open space where my brother and I had our bed. I could hear my mother praying the Act of Contrition into her dying aunt's ears. A few days later my father would accompany her body on the train back to Trenton.

It was years later, sometime after my father's own death, that my mother would speak of the day she received that letter from her great aunt. She didn't know what to think. We were poor and our house was very small. She recounted how she passed the letter to my father to see what he would say. He slowly read the letter, then turned to my mother and said, "How can we tell her she can't come?"

Just writing those words brings tears to my eyes. Hearing them may have brought tears to my mother's eyes. There was obvious pride in her voice as she shared this. Dad's words had touched her deeply. She repeated them with so much admiration for the way her husband had responded to her elderly aunt's plea for help. This was her aunt, not his, but that hadn't mattered at all. This woman needed a place to spend whatever time she had left. He knew they had to tell her to come.

*July 18, 2013*

*D*ear Ellamae,

100, that's enough! Yes, it was. You had every right to decide it was time to let go. Sure, we would all have loved to keep you here longer, but we completely understand that you felt you had reached the finish line. Like St. Paul, you had fought the good fight, you had finished the race, you had kept the faith. You knew you would be on the podium.

Margaret and I feel so blessed that we got to see you just five days before you took leave of this earth. We could tell that you were tired, that you were slowing down. Life was less fun now. But you were glad to see us and we were so glad to see you. You were looking forward to a visit from Shirley in a few weeks and made a point of steering us to your room so you could show us the note with the date of her arrival. Just knowing that she would be here soon was already making you happy. We were touched by your concern that there was no mention of Ken in the note. You hoped that he was okay, that he wasn't sick and unable to come. Right to the end you were looking out for others, for those you loved.

I like to recall special moments from years ago and some from the recent past. Back in early 1973 you took the train to Toronto with my mother so she could be at our daughter Michelle's baptism. I don't think my mother would have been there had you not said you wanted to come too. You and your Aunt Bessie were very close. It was special to have you both there that day. I recall another moment from just a few years ago. Margaret and I were having lunch with you at Lanark Lodge in our own little area the staff had prepared for us. A male resident came up to the table pushing his walker and just stood there. He was in no hurry to move on. When he did leave you told us that he had wanted to get a little place somewhere that you and he could move into together. It didn't seem that you had much difficulty declining the offer. The attraction was not that mutual. However, I did admire his taste in older women. That gave me a good excuse to tease you about male friends in our later visits. I would ask if you had any new boyfriends. You would laugh out loud and say very emphatically, "No! I'm too old for that!"

Now I want to get serious for just a minute, Ellamae. A man by the name of Léon Bloy who lived in France around the time that you were born once wrote: "There are places in the heart that do not yet exist; suffering has to enter in for them to come to be." He must have had people like you in mind. You have known way more than your share of suffering in your long life. Suffering that could have soured you on life, could have turned you into a sad and bitter person in your later years. Losing your husband and your father on one tragic night would have broken many a person. Would have taken all the joy out of living and left them forever despondent. But that is not what happened with you. Even more tender and loving places came to life in that beautiful heart of yours. It took time, but the light in your eyes eventually grew bright again and your laugh became fuller and even more delightful. Your strong faith in God carried you through this dark night of the soul.

Thank you, Ellamae, for the times you led us to that dear old house on Tennyson Road where my mother and your father and their brothers were born. And where you were perhaps born as well. Margaret and I were there again this past July and we hope to return as often as we can. You will be with us each time we do.

God speed, dear cousin. We love you.

*August 27, 2016*

# Through a Crack

She doggedly pushed her head across the floor. That was how she crawled. How else were you supposed to move from one side of a room to the other if you were not strong enough to lift your head? She would do that for a whole year till she was finally able to raise her head. Then she would keep on crawling till she was two and a half, with her head sometimes hitting the floor with a clunk when she grew tired and weaker at the end of the day. If she cried at those moments, you knew that the floor where we happened to be was a particularly hard one. She was tough.

Our feelings of pity often gave way to feelings of admiration for this child who showed such determination not to let her disabilities hold her back. She was who she was, and she would do whatever she had to do to get where she wanted to go. I would look at her and think to myself, *Christine, you have the same right to be here as the rest of us.* And I spoke of her in those days as a flower growing up through a crack in the sidewalk. It's not supposed to be there. But it is! It simply is. Life asserting itself against the odds.

Saying to all who pass, "Do you love me? I love you. Can we be friends?"

*August 1, 2016*

$O$ur daughter Christine was born with CHARGE Syndrome. Because of this, Christine, who is now thirty-eight, has a number of what people call "disabilities." Though she has some usable vision, she was born legally blind and hearing impaired. She has been completely deaf for the past several years. Christine is highly intelligent and possesses a phenomenal memory.

One of the characteristics of people like our daughter is that they lack the normal inhibitions that govern much of human interaction. They tend to say exactly what they think. They tell it like it is. They don't mean to offend anyone; it just never occurs to them that people would be hurt by hearing the truth. There are times when I see this dis-ability as being the exact opposite: a unique a-bility.

Christine prefers not to join us on occasions when there will be several people present. Because she cannot hear anything that is being said, she finds large gatherings very frustrating, so we will often go over to her group home for a private celebration of special events. This is why I was spending a few hours with her on the day after Father's Day. She wanted to give me a card and a present and have some father/daughter time.

The handwritten card turned out to be a far greater present than the beautiful shirt she gave me. Keenly aware that this was just three weeks after my eightieth birthday, she wrote: "I hope to spend more time with you since you won't be around much longer." I burst out laughing. That tends to be the reaction of most people with whom I share this story. One of my friends described her comment as "priceless." And that is how I see it too.

Thank you, Christine, for this refreshing reminder of what is so obvious. My time here really is growing shorter. As you sometimes say, in your very matter-of-fact manner, we have to die and move on to make room for the others who are arriving. I love the shirt you gave me. I love even more this other gift, your stark reminder that my time here with you and all those I love is not endless. I too, at some point before long, will have to move on and make room for the others. Till then, I do hope to spend more time with you.

*June 18, 2013*

*N*ear our very modest house in the town where I grew up lived a family that consisted of a middle-aged couple, one or two of their adult children, and frequently other people who seemed to come and go. Often on a Saturday night there would be wild parties with a lot of drinking and shouting of obscenities. In the summer one could sometimes detect a foul odour coming from that house. Cleanliness did not seem to be high on their list of priorities. I can still remember the day the bailiff and his men arrived to evict them, apparently for not keeping up their rent payments. Neighbours stood in their doorways watching as the contents of the house were carried out and placed on the sidewalk. I've never forgotten the sound of the woman's voice as she screamed at the men who were moving out her family's belongings. By evening the house was empty and the bailiff had changed the locks on the doors. The spectacle was over, and those who had been taking all this in, while trying not to be seen gawking, pulled down their blinds or closed their doors and went inside.

The next thing I knew, my father and mother were inviting this man and his wife and one of their adult children to move into our small place. They stayed with us for a few weeks. No explanation for my parents' decision was ever given to me or my younger brother or sister. Perhaps they felt we were too young to understand. It was only years later that I realized the full significance of what they had done. Without any words at all, and in a manner far more powerful than words, my parents had shown us what it means to see all others as persons, regardless of their appearance or the circumstances of their lives. They recognized that these less-than-ideal neighbours were made in the same image and likeness as the rest of us.

*March 11, 2012*

"*T*hank you for this visit," he said. How was I to know that those would be the last words he would say to me before his stroke a few weeks later?

It was early November 1967, and I had come home for my mother's birthday. She was fifteen years younger than her husband, but he had always seemed to be the stronger of the two. They had married late. He was forty-nine when he fathered me into existence. After only sixteen years by their side, I said goodbye to them and the younger brother and sister they had given me. This short visit was but one of so many that ended all too soon. Yet he wasn't complaining that I had to leave once more. He was simply grateful that I had come home for my mother's birthday, that I had spent a few days in their company. Gratitude for whatever precious time we had together was more his style than any complaining about my having to go away again. "Thank you for this visit" came so naturally to his lips. I knew how much he meant it, and so those words have never left me. They never will.

Why is it only later that we realize the full import of these moments? Are not all our goodbyes both bitter and sweet? We do not know which ones are the last in a series we assume has no end. Then we try to go back and gather up all the crumbs of tenderness and meaning we left lying on the floor that day. But the REWIND button doesn't work like that. Life is always on PLAY, and that is the only option we are given. Thank God for memory that does its best to bring us back in time to soak up all the love our busy lives kept us from tasting to the full when we were there.

To all those I hold dear, I say: "Thank you for this visit. Thank you for visiting my life with your friendship, and for each moment we spent together on the journey. May our last visit not really be the last."

*September 5, 2008*

# It Doesn't Matter

"It doesn't matter what happens now," she told her neighbour on that January day in 1982. Just a few days earlier she had received the answer to her prayers. Her son's wife had given birth to a baby boy, and he would be called Jim. There would be another James Small. The husband she had lost fifteen years earlier would not be forgotten. His name would go on. At the age of eighty-three, her life now seemed complete.

No wonder her brother said she had "pranced around the kitchen like a teenager" the evening she received the news her heart longed for. She was the one who had hoped for a boy even more than anyone else had. A male child would be named after his grandfather, she had been told, and that thought had filled her heart with deep joy and anticipation. Now the moment had arrived and her happiness could not be contained. It didn't matter what happened now.

How many of us will know such a Simeon experience? A joy so total, so overwhelming, that we will feel it is time to go. That our life has run its course and our time here cannot hold anything more. Thirteen days after our son was born, my mother got up, had a breakfast of toast and tea, then lay down on the sofa and closed her eyes for the last time. Did she really die from heart failure? Could it instead have been from a heart so full and so at peace that she just let go?

*December 29, 2010*

# The God of My Father

(Excerpts from a paper on "The Fatherhood of God," written
for the course "Le Mystère de Dieu," Laval University,
April 1985. God, as pure Spirit, is beyond gender and
can just as accurately be referred to as Mother.)

*H*e was fifty years old when I, the first of his three children, was born. Sixteen years later, with his blessing upon me, I followed what seemed to be a call from God to leave my father's house. Never again would I spend more than a few days at a time in his presence. Yet no other person has so deeply marked my life or had such an influence upon my faith. There is no doubt that when I call God Father, I am in no small way unconsciously evoking the memory of my own father. Often I wonder how all this happened and how it happened in so short a time.

\*\*\*

At the time of my father's eightieth birthday, I tried to describe in a letter to a friend my deep awareness of the profound connection between my father's existence and my own. What struck me on that occasion was the intimate and unique relationship between his bodily presence in the universe and my body/spirit existence in time and eternity. How not only my physical self but even certain qualities of mind and heart had traveled across that microscopic bridge between his being and mine. I thought of the mysterious way in which a tiny particle of matter from his body had been the vehicle by which I had come to receive this breath of life carried down the centuries of time. And so I wrote: "From his body, vivified by his soul, came the seed that sparked eternally the life that breathes in me." Despite an apparent dualism of body and soul, the statement shows a Teilhardian awareness that these miniscule particles of the visible world bear within them traces of the invisible, and that matter is already infused with spirit. It was precisely this interpenetration of matter and spirit that I was trying to capture in that sentence. What fascinated me was the mysterious link between this tiny element from my father's body—joined to one from my mother's body—and my existence as more than body, as body/spirit. I sensed that his seed was alive with the *ruah* of God, and I knew that my journey had begun there. To trace my origin to my father was also to trace it to my God. It has always seemed natural to call both of them Father.

***

An essential part of my paternal image is the combining of strength with dependence upon God. One of my most enduring memories is the sight of my father on his knees beside his bed in prayer, oblivious to all around him. My mother prayed too, perhaps even more than my father, but it was the sight of this big, strong man kneeling before his God in silent prayer that touched me deeply. Whatever sense I have of a transcendent, holy Being can be traced in large part to that quiet witness. Faith was not weakness. It was the simple acknowledgment that one was not the author of one's own existence. I learned very early and forever the difference between the Creator and the creature.

***

We all have certain moments in time stamped indelibly in our consciousness. My father's death is one such moment. He was almost eighty-five, at the end of a long and hard but happy life. He had been sick for only two weeks. The stroke had taken its toll, and now he lay unconscious in his hospital bed. We felt that this might be his last night. I took my mother home; she was at the point of exhaustion. In the middle of the night I awakened and returned alone to stand by my father's bed, to hold his hand one last time. Fifteen minutes later he died. I watched in awe the countdown of his final breaths, those breaths that he had first begun to draw well over three-quarters of a century before. Now they had come to an end. He was gone.

A strange peace came over me and a question, a wonder, flooded my consciousness. The question was not "Where had he gone?" Not "Why did he have to die?" The question that cried out for an answer was "What unspeakably marvelous Being could possibly be the Source of the goodness and the beauty I had known in this man?" It was his life, not his death, that demanded an explanation. Not "Why did he have to die?" but rather "Why had he ever been?" was the question. What Ultimate Existence could explain his? What other

Goodness could explain this one? What infinite Beauty did this one reflect? One final time my father had put starkly before my eyes the question that his whole life had been for me: "Where have I come from? Who is my Father?"

# *Postscript*

## On Turning Eighty

Good evening, good people!

Let me begin with a brief story that Margaret can verify is true. At the end of April, just a few days after we had returned from California, I woke up one morning in a state of panic. My first thought that morning was *How are we going to feed all those people coming to the party?* Here was my very next thought: *I know what I'll do. I'll just show up with a couple of loaves of bread and a few fish and ask Deacon Randy if he can help us out.* Aren't you glad, Randy, that we came up with another plan?

As many of you know, one of the reasons for our trip to California was to celebrate Margaret's mother's ninetieth birthday. And now here we are celebrating my eightieth. The math is not difficult. When our daughter Michelle was in elementary school, she used to love to say to her friends, "My grandparents were ten when my father was born." They would quickly assure her that that simply wasn't possible. And then she would explain why it definitely was possible, and very true.

So it was yesterday I hit the big 8-O mark. It is so very fitting that this party is taking place the following day, on May 25. You see, today is the anniversary of my parents' wedding. I used to love to tease them: "So I arrived on May 24 and the two of you decided the next day that maybe you should get married." As you may have guessed, I was born on the eve of their first anniversary. Quite the anniversary present! Even if I arrived unwrapped, with nothing but a cord attached. So these two dates are more than a little significant in my personal history. Without my mom and dad's May 25, there would have been no May 24 for me. No me, period. God needed their help.

Have you ever let your mind wander back in time to all those ancestors of yours, those people in your past who had to meet, and fall in love, and choose life together, for you to come to be? Have you ever breathed a little prayer of gratitude to them? Hope I get to meet all of mine someday and get the chance to say thanks.

If you were to ask me to describe how I feel as I reach this milestone in my life, I would respond in one word: grateful. I am so very, very grateful. Not simply for reaching eighty, however, but for the fact that I ever came to be at all. That is the mystery that each of us lives with: Why me? Why was I given this gift that underlies all other gifts? Sometimes I think about the fact that God had to give me to me before there was any me. I guess that's what it means to be called out of nothingness. And God had to give you to you before anyone else could give you anything. We are all on loan to ourselves, and I find it so freeing to live with that awareness. It leaves me so very, very grateful.

Some of you have heard me express the view that we should all be going around in a state of awe most of the time. Just over the fact that we *are*, and that we inhabit this amazing Earth, this tiny pearl nestled in one little corner of a mind-blowing universe that is so vast we seem incapable of even beginning to comprehend how endless it may be. And we have been given the immense privilege of being part of the conscious dimension of this universe, with all the nobility and responsibility that goes with that. It seems to me (and at eighty I claim the right to express my opinion) that we fail to fully appreciate the nobility of our calling as humans, and we fail to fully accept our responsibility for one another and all life on this planet we call our home. It's not that there aren't other forms of life that have varying degrees of consciousness and emotions. We had a dog for twelve years, so we know what they and other animals can teach us. Shadow would tear around the house with unbridled delight whenever we returned after a few days away. But we humans, we are the poets and the artists and the philosophers and the musicians and the scientists. We know and know that we know. We love and know that we love. We are gifted beyond anything that we could ever have dreamed up for ourselves. Today's "in" word *awesome* does not come close to capturing the wonder and the majesty of it all. We really should be going around in a state of awe and gratitude most of the time. We might not get much done that way, but perhaps we would all be happier and less inclined to start wars.

Now here's where I get myself in trouble. Margaret reminded me that five years ago I wrote a piece for her and read it to all of you who were there on that occasion. No need to focus on her again was the message. At the risk of incurring her displeasure, I have to say something on this occasion about the woman with whom I have shared more than half of these eighty years.

Not every woman, a mere eighteen months into her marriage and pregnant with her first child, would agree to spend the next two years living in a group home to help some teenagers who needed a stable environment. Our daughter Michelle was born our first Christmas there, and we sometimes joke that the reason she became a lawyer was because her mother carried her into court so often during the first months of her life. Some of those teenagers had regular visits there. Not every woman would have agreed, a few years after that experience and now with two young children, one of whom had been born with significant physical challenges, to move into another group home, this time one for single moms. I had attended a workshop for religion teachers where we discussed a newly released document of the Canadian Catholic bishops entitled *A Society to Be Transformed*. I came home and said to Margaret, "What would you think of moving into another group home to help some young people?" She didn't even ask for a few days to think about it. We spent six years in that residence, with Margaret being the only one at home during the day most of the time and the one who was there with the women in the hospital as they gave birth. And by the way, during our fifth year there she gave birth at home, with a doctor present, to our son Jim, who drove from Texas to be here this evening. And now Margaret is chair of the board of Lions McInnes House in Brantford, where Christine lives. She donates hours of her time on behalf of our daughter and the other residents of this fine home for adults who are deafblind.

Margaret, how could I not love you? How could I not admire you? How could I not be proud of you? Go ahead and give me heck for speaking of you again. It is my birthday, you know. Thanks for saying yes to spending your life with me. And with our children: Michelle, the mother of our three amazing grandchildren (thanks for your role in that, Bart—you too, Heather and Peter); Christine, our second child, who reminds us that life is really all about loving and being loved—plus some jewelry, of course; and Jim, our Texan, who thinks the best thing I ever did for him was get him an American mother. A passport sure beats having to get a green card. I still miss all those nights I spent in hockey rinks with you, Jim. I even enjoyed the practices. Michelle, since you became part of the legal team at TD

Canada Trust, whenever I pass a TD bank I feel as though I'm a part owner. Even though it's they who own us.

Two of our offspring did not make it to birth. However, they were a part of us for a significant period of time, one for three months and another for four months. We do not know why such things happen. Once in a while I think of them and wish they too had been around our family table. Will we get to meet them someday? That we do not know, but I like to think that kind of lovely surprise may await us down the road.

It is very special to have a number of former students here this evening. It was a privilege years ago to have you in my class, and I am honoured that you are here on this occasion. It has been so great to have you become lifelong friends. I can't tell you how much that has meant to me. Margaret and I were at some of your weddings. We have broken bread together in your homes. Thanks, Carolann, for recently posting a TED Talk by an amazing educator in the States. Listening to that inspiring woman brought tears to my eyes and made me wish I could start my teaching career all over again and do an even better job next time. I loved teaching and I loved spending my days with such wonderful young people. Thank you for the privilege, and thank you for being here.

All you good people here this evening—the young, those in the middle of your journey, those who are senior citizens like myself—you are all what I like to call the beautiful landscape of my life. In some cases long stretches of our lives have matched each other's almost year for year; in other cases only parts of our lives will overlap. It does not matter. We are here on this Earth at this same moment in history, and our paths have crossed in a meaningful way. I am grateful for each of you. I am glad that you, too, were given life. Of all those who have ever lived, you are the ones with whom I am privileged to share my time here. You are more precious to me than anything one can purchase in a store. Those things cannot be my friends. Only you can. And I love you all.

*May 25, 2013*

# Acknowledgments

$A$ heartfelt thanks to all of you who have in any way at any time encouraged me to publish my reflections. It was the cumulative effect of your many voices that finally convinced me to attempt this book. You know who you are. If anyone finds inspiration or meaning in these pages, that person is indebted to you as well.

My friend Diane Durran deserves a very special mention. For twenty-three years she kept insisting that the reflection I sent to her back in 1994 should be published. She was sure that my response to her remark in a phone conversation contained a message that would be of benefit to many others. It has taken me this long to accept that she may be right. Thanks, Diane, for not giving up on me. You had to badger me at times, but without you this book might never have come to be.

Christine O'Brien also merits her own thank-you. When I inserted a few of my reflections into a speech on my 70th birthday, she took my wife aside to say that those pieces were "publishable." Her comment surprised me, and I filed it away as a source of encouragement. A few years ago she was the one to whom I would send new pieces of writing to get her feedback. I owe you, Christine. And I owe your husband Tom, who read my entire manuscript and has given me other support as well on various occasions. I still remember the time he casually remarked that I had "a way with words." That, coming from an Irishman with no small measure of the eloquence of his people, meant more than he realized.

I owe another Irishman, my friend Patrick Gallagher, a huge debt of gratitude. He brought his keen mind and extensive background in philosophy and theology to bear on every word of my manuscript, and wrote copious notes on everything he observed. Patrick pointed out places where my words could be taken in ways I had not intended, leading me to make important changes. I am deeply indebted to you, Pat. My readers are too.

Mary Redmond is a member of our theology discussion group. She readily agreed to read my manuscript and she too provided me with pages of written comments. I am grateful to you, Mary, for the time you so generously devoted to evaluating each piece of my writing, giving me important feedback and suggesting ways to organize my work. Your thoughtful observations were a great help to me.

How many writers, as they struggle to put out their first book, have the good fortune to have an artist and former member of the Graphic Design Faculty of Sheridan College come along one fine day and graciously offer their services? John Elphick, how can I ever thank you for all the hours, adding up to days, that you spent writing out detailed instructions regarding font, spacing, interior layout, and making drawings of possible covers? This book is yours as well as mine. Thank you for your friendship and the precious gift of your talent and your time. I'm sure the staff of Friesen Press were grateful for all your help.

Thank you, John Kuypers, for the witness of your faith, the example of your own writing, and your appreciation of mine.

I wish to acknowledge Kate Marshall Flaherty, award-winning author of several books of poetry. Your public readings are always a source of inspiration to me. Thank you for your friendship and the support that only a fellow writer can give.

Robert and Susan Morgan, dear friends of many years and our son's godparents, have both affirmed me in my writing on numerous occasions. Robert still performs Morgan's Journey, the longest running touring play in Canadian history. Susan has been recognized for the compassion and sensitivity she brings to her ministry to the dying, in particular those who have chosen to live out their last days at home. My sincere thanks to the two of you for years of friendship and the many ways you have encouraged me as a writer.

It was from the shores of Anna Maria Island in Florida that I first submitted samples of my reflections to Friesen Press. Thank you, Jim and Carolann Malenfant, for introducing us to that beautiful oasis. And thank you for the many times you have expressed your appreciation of the pieces of writing I have shared with you. Your friendship is a precious part of our lives.

"Margaret, which of these sounds better?" How often over the years have I asked my dear wife to help me decide which was the better word or phrase to express a certain thought? I always trusted her judgment. She would know if one way was better than the other. Your own fine literary sense runs through these pages, Margaret. I am grateful for more than that, however. There were times during these past few years when it was you who kept me on task. I know that I tested your patience at times as I took forever to get through certain stages of this endeavour. Thank you for coming to my rescue on those occasions and offering to put all the pieces of writing into a single format, or into logical groupings, or to contact publishers for permission to use a quotation. This is very much *our book*.

As some of you may have read on the back cover, I left home at the age of sixteen to join the De La Salle Christian Brothers, a worldwide Catholic teaching order. I wish to acknowledge here the immense debt I owe to that fine religious congregation. Had the Brothers not come to my small hometown when they did, I doubt that I would have completed high school, and I almost certainly would not have become a teacher. They became my second parents and set me on a path to higher learning and spiritual formation that otherwise would have been beyond my means or aspirations. I owe them more than I can say. Being a member of the Lasallian family has been such an important part of my own journey *on the way to here*.

Finally, I wish to express my deep gratitude to all those at Friesen Press who have guided this first-time author through all the stages of publishing a book. From my initial contacts with Kim Schacht and Dawn Johnston to my frequent and lengthy exchanges with Judith Hewlett, my Author Account Manager, you have all been so professional and encouraging and helpful. Margaret knows how often I have said, "I must get in touch with Judith about that." I feel especially grateful to my copy editor, Rosemary Wilson, not only for her excellent editing skills, but in particular for allowing me to use her personal testimonial on the cover of my book. Your words touched and inspired me, Rosemary. Thank you. And thank you to the excellent design department at Friesen Press for a book that they and I can be proud of.

*Burlington, Ontario*
*July 1, 2017*